Living the Southwest Lifestyle

How to Have and Maintain Peace of Mind

Matthew C. Cox

Living the Southwest Lifestyle – How to Have and Maintain Peace of Mind

ISBN-13: 978-0615472119
ISBN-10: 0615472117

Library of Congress Control Number: 2011905367

Published by Peace of Mind Training Institute Publishing

©Copyright 2011
Second Printing 2011
Matthew C. Cox

All rights reserved. No part of this book may be used or reproduced in any manner whatsoever without written permission of Matthew C. Cox, except in the case of brief quotations embodied in critical articles and reviews.

For information, contact:

    Peace of Mind Training Institute
    21 Pine Ridge Road
    Sandia Park, NM 87047
    505-286-9567 info@PeaceofMindTrainingInstitute.com

Acknowledgements

There are a several people who made significant contributions as we finalized this version of the book. These include Diana Massengale, who created beautiful artwork and cover design and Stacey Brown, who took over many of my other responsibilities so I could finish this task.

I'm especially grateful to Sheri Cox, who has never failed in her belief of our life purpose together and who coordinated this project to bring it to reality.

The number of people who contributed to Living the Southwest Lifestyle is beyond my capability to remember or acknowledge. This work took more than eight years of my life to put together and it encompasses all of my experiences from my earliest memory to the recent present. If you know me, you contributed to this work and I thank you. If you recognize yourself in one of the stories or examples in this book, I especially thank you. If you recognize yourself and feel my representation of you is unfavorable, please understand that I know you did your best and I am grateful for the influence you had in my story.

Table of Contents

Foreword i

Introduction ii

How to Have and Maintain Peace of Mind 1

The Miracle of A Hidden Car 60

Personal Peace of Mind 63

Questions and Answers about Virtual Mentors 104

Listening to My Desire and Intuition 107

Relationship Peace of Mind 115

More Information on Nakedness 168

Financial Peace of Mind 173

Q and A about Releasing Resistance 237

What is the Next Step on My Journey to Peace of Mind? 241

Foreword

How to Use this Book

This is a "how-to" book. Of course, since each person's learning style is different, I realize the teaching style of this material may not coincide with your personal learning style. Therefore, this forward offers you a few tips as you seek to apply Peace of Mind Training to your life.

This book was originally written as four individual booklets. The first booklet offers an overview of the material, including brief descriptions of the three universal laws that serve as a basis for Peace of Mind Training. Each of the next three sections goes into greater detail for each law. As a result, there is some repetition in the material. This repetition may be tedious to you. However, it serves a purpose. It reinforces the message so you can more easily remember it. I invite you to lean into the repetition and allow it to speak to you at the place where you are at today. My observation is that I often receive new insights when I experience something more than once. I suspect this will be true for you as well.

Each chapter concludes with Conspiracy Questions. I explain these questions in the material so I won't repeat that explanation here. However, I encourage you to take the time to answer each question completely. If you want to purchase a workbook for this purpose, you may do so through our website. If you want to print your own, we offer a PDF on the website that you may download free of charge. Just visit www.ltswls.com and click on Peace Seeker Workbook in the right hand column.

If you prefer to experience this material in an audio or video format, I encourage you to visit our website to see if these projects are complete. Our intent is to make these formats available as soon as possible. However, at the time of publication of this book, we did not have a timeline set for these projects.

Best wishes on your journey to Peace of Mind.

Matthew C. Cox

Introduction

I have an innate Desire to live with Peace of Mind.

This Desire is selfish because I know that individual Peace of Mind leads to world peace and I prefer world peace to world war.

This book is my personal story of discovery of how I learned to have and maintain Peace of Mind. I share it with the intent to help others discover Peace of Mind so we may experience world peace in our lifetime.

My story starts in the mid 1980s. Sheri and I are living in North Carolina when we receive the call, the pull, and the urge to move to the Southwestern United States

So, in April of 1987, we pack up our twin baby boys and our possessions to move west.

The lifestyle we find in New Mexico is different from anything we previously experienced.

It brings Peace of Mind to our Personal Life, Relationships, and Finances. However, we don't know why it brings Peace of Mind.

Is it the Native American culture?
Is it the open spaces?
Is it the climate?

We don't know so we start reading. We explore teachings, seminars, books, live presentations, and recordings.

Our goal is to identify why so we can share it with those around us and we can all experience Peace of Mind.

Through this research, we discover three laws. These are Universal Laws. They are:

1. The Law of Miracles
2. The Law of Attraction
3. The Law of Abundance

We observe that these laws receive more acceptance in the Southwestern United States than in other places we have lived. As a result, we call using these laws "Living the Southwest Lifestyle."

This book explores these laws and our story.

It is the result of our search for four things that religion is suppose to provide.

1. Integrity
2. Openness
3. Purity
4. Peace of Mind

I spend the first thirty-five years of my life in organized religion looking for these characteristics. I cannot find them.

I figure I am the problem so I become more devoted, pray more, and study more.

Still, I cannot find what I seek.

Then, one day, I have an epiphany. It comes from a single question.

"How can a God that is love rule His people by fear?"

As I seek the answer to that question, I find everything I am looking for and much more.

This book, divided in four sections, uses true events from my life to define the Universal Laws we discovered in New Mexico and to describe how I found what I sought.

Section One is an overview of how we discovered the three laws. Sections Two through Four examine each law through dramatic true stores. These stories show you how The Law of Miracles, The Law of Attraction, and The Law of Abundance work to give you Peace of Mind.

Introduction

One of the basic teachings of Peace of Mind Training Institute is that Peace of Mind is part of a Conspiracy. You may find the term "Conspiracy" a bit spooky unless you understand the conspiracy is in your favor (and mine).

When you explore Peace of Mind teaching, you discover life is a "Conspiracy for Me". You will smile when you see that not only do all things work together for good, all things work together by design for your benefit (and mine and everyone's!).

Therefore, to help you identify the Universe's Conspiracy for you, each chapter has a Conspiracy Question to answer.

The best way to get the most out of each Conspiracy Question is to write down the answer. You may do this in a notebook.

If you have comments, questions, or wish to share this material with others, please see the Contact Information in the back of this book.

Living the Southwest Lifestyle

How to Have and Maintain Peace of Mind

The Law of Miracles

Chapter 1

I arrive home from work on a late winter afternoon in 1985. I hurriedly clean the trailer I call home. Mom and Dad are driving four hours from their home in Southern Virginia to visit me in North Carolina. They will visit for a couple of days.

Tonight they will have dinner with me and a friend named Sheri. They arrive and we catch up on what has happened since we last visited. The conversation turns to our guest for the evening. I explain that she is working with me on a song. I casually mention her father's upcoming job transfer to Albuquerque, New Mexico. I say that the family will move there within the year.

It is just conversation. I have no hidden meaning or agenda behind my words.

My mother immediately says, "If the wedding is there, we won't be able to attend."

I am shocked. I haven't even thought of marrying our evening's scheduled guest. I certainly do not consider our relationship a dating relationship.

My job includes interacting with numerous other singles my age and I normally invite one or more of them to join me when my parents come to visit. I am an only child and having another person around brings variety to my parents' visits. There is no reason for my mother to say what she said.

My shock turns to confusion. Maybe I didn't hear her accurately. Maybe she misspoke. I ask, "What wedding?"

Mom looks up as if awaken from a dream and says, "Oh, never mind."

I drop the subject but I remember the conversation. I still vividly remember it today.

Flash forward a few weeks.

It is the morning of March 31, 1985. The North Carolina sun shines into my room and wakes me. I stretch and I stay in bed. I am somewhere between unconscious and conscious when the voice inside my head speaks.

"Today is the day you will ask Sheri's Dad to marry her."

I experience emotions of fear, elation, and panic. I have known Sheri and her family for only three months. Larry, her Dad, is a master intimidator and I am not sure I know how to approach him on the subject of marrying his daughter. I respond.

"How will I start the conversation?"

"Don't worry," says the voice, "It will be obvious."

My emotional state stabilizes as I realize that if what the voice told me is true, I just have to show up and everything will take care of itself.

I am not aware of it at the time but I am experiencing something very normal. It is called The Law of Miracles.

> **Conspiracy for Me!**
>
> *Through this book, you will learn that Peace of Mind is part of a Conspiracy. You may find the term "Conspiracy" a bit spooky unless you understand the conspiracy is in your favor (and mine).*
>
> *You will discover that life is a "Conspiracy for Me". You will smile when you see that not only do all things work together for good, all things work together by design for your benefit (and mine and everyone's!)*
>
> *At the end of Chapter 2, I'll tell you how we'll help you identify how life is a Conspiracy for You!*

Chapter 2

The Law of Miracles states that Miracles occur naturally as expressions of love.

By definition, a Miracle is a supernatural shortcut through time and space that happens because of love. Miracles flow naturally and produce supernatural results.

Miracles are not Magic. Magic puts pressure on someone to perform by generating his or her own energy.

There is a big difference between Magic and Miracles. First, let's look at Magic.

The dictionary describes "Magic" as the art that controls natural events by invoking the supernatural.

Look closer at that definition and you see that "supernatural" is really just another term for those things that happen outside of our five natural senses.

As science develops a greater ability to observe brainwaves, subatomic particles, and other previously unseen matter, science redefines supernatural. What once appeared supernatural is now natural because we understand that life functions at a molecular level.

The Law of Magic operates at the molecular level.

The Law of Magic is incremental and logical. The results appear to be Magic but they aren't.

Just like a magician's trick, the results are easy to explain with a modest understanding of molecular science. In fact, I explain them in my writing about the Law of Attraction.

The Law of Miracles operates at the molecular level too. In addition, it operates at the quantum level.

The Law of Miracles is non-incremental and it feels illogical. It is not as predictable as The Law of Magic and more difficult to explain.

The Law of Miracles is the supreme law and it always works for your benefit.

It may seem complex. However, it is simple to understand when broken down into three elements.

They are:

1. Understand Desire
2. Use Thoughts, Words, Actions and Habits to Receive Your Desire
3. Know You Always Do Your Best

> **Conspiracy Question**
>
> *To help you identify the Universe's Conspiracy for you, most Chapters have a Conspiracy Question to answer.*
>
> *The best way to get the most out of each Conspiracy Question is to write down the answer. You may do this in a notebook.*

Chapter 3

ELEMENT ONE: Understand Desire

The Law of Miracles works from the point of Desire - your Desire. Do you know what you want from life? Have you taken the time to search your heart and discover your Desire?

Some religions teach that Desire might be bad. Others say that Desire is sinful or selfish.

The truth is "Desire" comes from the Latin word meaning "of the Father." If you have a Desire, your God put that Desire into you. It is sacred. It is holy.

That Desire may be your final destination or it may be a stepping-stone to get to your final destination. Either way, it is there because you need to fulfill it to experience the design for your life.

Finding your Desire is Miraculous because it is God speaking to you. God gives you the Desire. God then gives you what you need to fulfill it. That gift consists of your talents and abilities combined with external events, including the fulfillment of other people's Desire.

I remember when I discovered my Desire ...

In the summer of 1984, I attend a seminar in the Baltimore, Maryland Civic Center. As I listen to the material, a Desire grows within me. It impresses me. It excites me. It emotionally charges me.

More than twenty years later, this Desire is still with me. It is a driving, compelling Desire. It is the Desire of creating a family of fifty people in three generations to make the world a better place.

As the Desire ignites within me, the seminar speaker says that as few as two or three committed people have changed the entire course of human history. He lists world leaders such as George Washington, Benjamin Franklin, Adolph Hitler, Winston Churchill, and others.

I ask myself, "What would happen with fifty people completely committed to a course of action?

Would it affect the world? Would it create social change? Would it give hope to the world?" I know the answer is "yes."

I wonder if fifty people in three generations is possible. I do the math.

First, find a wife with the same Desire.

Then, have eight children - educate them at home and prepare them for the next step.

Next, those eight children find eight people with the same Desire. Those eight couples have an average of four children each.

Two people, my wife and I, plus eight children is ten. Add eight spouses to make 18. Eight families with an average of four children per family is 32. Add the 32 to 18 and you have fifty.

It is possible.

I realize it might not work out exactly that way but the numbers work.

It is a Desire born out of love - a Miracle.

> **Conspiracy Question**
>
> *What is my Desire?*

Chapter 4

ELEMENT TWO: Use Thoughts, Words, Actions, and Habits to Receive Your Desire

Receiving your Desire is easy. It is natural... unless you create resistance.

For the twenty-three years prior to my experience in Baltimore, I learn to resist.

My religion teaches me to resist things I enjoy because they might be "bad."

Even the things I know are "good" become difficult because of my resistance habit.

I habitually blame others for my struggles. I habitually live as a victim. I habitually create enemies. I habitually see barriers in everyone and everything.

Those habits stand between my Desire and me. I finally understand that to fulfill my Desire, I must change my habits.

To change habits, I must understand habits. I devote much of my free time to learning how to change my behavior.

I learn that at least eighty percent of my actions are habitual. The way I dress myself, how I get into bed at night, my speech patterns, and the way I brush my teeth are all behavioral habits.

If I carry on a conversation while driving my car, I participate in the habitual behavior of driving. I don't consciously think about the foot pressure I'm putting on the gas pedal or how much I have to turn the steering wheel to go around a corner. I do it by habit.

Those habits don't just happen. I program those habits through repetitive actions.

In addition, my life depends upon some habits. My heart and lungs function by habit. I have certain inborn instincts that qualify behavior habits. These include blinking, smiling, scowling, and flinching. God programs those habits.

Once a habit forms, I do not have to be consciously aware to perform it. Therefore, by definition, the subconscious part of my brain controls those habits.

Scientific studies show that the subconscious makes up 5/6 of the brain. That part of my brain (83% of it) controls my habits, which are at least 80% of my actions.

That means my brain uses only 17% of its capacity for conscious behavior. The rest of my brain controls and manages my habitual behavior.

This is a problem if I consciously decide to change a habitual behavior. Eighty-three percent of my brain controls the habit and seventeen percent controls the decision to change the habit. The seventeen percent puts up a good fight but it always loses to the eighty-three percent because it is outmanned.

It seems hopeless. It feels as if fate has given me a certain place in life and I can do nothing about it. Carl Jung (Yung) addressed this very issue when he said

> "Until you make the unconscious conscious, it will control your life and you will call it fate."

However, I learn that if I have programmed old habits into my subconscious, I can program NEW habits into my subconscious to replace the old ones.

I do this through using thoughts, words, and actions to develop new habits. Those thoughts, words, and actions become the tools I use to fulfill my Desire.

I think about all the details of my Desire. I close my eyes so I can easily feel the feelings, smell the smells, taste the tastes, and imagine all parts of my Desire.

I write statements describing situations where my Desire is reality. I write the feelings, describe the smells and tastes, and feel the emotions of having that Desire. I program my subconscious to think differently.

Those subconscious thoughts turn into words. I speak my written statements every day. I program myself to talk differently. Instead of creating resistance with my words, I relax. Instead of creating enemies, I speak words of love.

These words turn into new actions. Instead of building barriers, I remove them.

Those new actions turn into habits.

Behavior psychologists say it takes 21-30 days to develop a new habit. For me, some habits happen more quickly. Others take longer to develop.

One by one, I develop new habits. Each brings me closer to my Desire.

I don't know how this programming works. I just know that it works. My subconscious quits working against me.

(By the way, I eventually learn how this process works and I write about that in a later chapter.)

From the summer of 1984 until I meet Sheri in the winter of the same year, I think about my idea of a family of fifty. I talk about it with everyone.

I know I will do it - if I ever find someone to marry me who has the same Desire. I sometimes wonder if I will ever find a partner. Many potential choices quit seeing me after I talk about having eight children.

I feel guilty because I have to choose between great potential partners and my Desire. I blame my Desire because some relationships can go no further. I am afraid I will never find a partner with the same Desire.

I haven't yet learned that the Universe is efficient. If it gives me a Desire for something that I cannot fulfill by myself, it also gives that Desire to those who will help me fulfill it.

However, there is another, bigger lesson I must learn first.

> **Conspiracy Question**
>
> *What changes can I make to integrate my Thoughts, Words, and Actions so I can receive my Desire?*

Chapter 5

ELEMENT THREE: Know You Always Do Your Best

My feelings of guilt start to bog me down. I look for other people to blame. I am afraid I will never have my Desire.

Unknowingly, I find the greatest obstacles to using The Law of Miracles. Those obstacles are the emotions of guilt, blame, and fear.

Even though I have moments of freedom, I live with those emotions for years.

My religion teaches me freedom and bondage. I experience love and fear, forgiveness and guilt.

In the moments of bondage, fear, and guilt, the guilt is more than I can bear so I blame other people. My perceived mistakes haunt me as I live in the past.

In addition, I am afraid of repeating those mistakes. That fear is a self-fulfilling prophecy for my actions.

I make more mistakes, feel more guilt, blame more people, experience more fear, and repeat.

In the moments of freedom, love, and forgiveness, my life moves forward, ever so slowly.

After more than thirty-five years of this double-minded life, I learn a secret. This secret challenges much of what I think is true so it takes me a while to believe it and even longer to act on it.

However, when I believe it and start acting on it, I finally experience Peace of Mind. In addition, I experience love and the resulting Miracles!

The secret I learn is that I always do my best. There are no mistakes.

My best may change as I process stimuli in my environment. I learn more. I experience more. My best is different when I am tired as opposed to when rested. However, I always do my best in the present moment.

If this is true for me, this is true for other people also. They always do their best. Deep down, no one wants to make mistakes. No one wants to hurt other people. Everyone wants what is best for them and those around them.

Limited knowledge or limited perspective may encourage us to do something that could be interpreted as a mistake or that could be called harmful.

However, the truth is, we always do our best. I always do my best. You always do your best. Everybody always does his or her best.

As I learn this, I mean really learn it, I become free from guilt, blame, and fear.

If I always do my best and I don't make mistakes, there is no need for guilt.

In addition, if I am not guilty, there is no need to blame other people. The reason is they always do their best and they don't make mistakes either.

This way of thinking completely changes the way I look at forgiveness. When I know everyone does his or her best, I do not experience guilt so I can easily "forgive" myself.

In addition, since I no longer have a need to blame others, I can easily "forgive" others.

When the guilt and blame disappear, fear disappears too. I discover a

side benefit. I learn how to love.

I demonstrate love whenever I am present in the moment. If I am not guilty about the past or blaming someone about the past or worrying about the future, I can remain present in the moment.

This becomes clear to me early one morning as the sun casts a glow behind the San Pedro Mountains out the east window of my office.

I work diligently. My wife Sheri brings me a cup of coffee and places it on the coaster on my desk. I'm in a writing zone. Everything is clicking. I barely acknowledge her for fear of breaking my zone.

A few minutes later, I reach for the coffee and discover the coaster is stuck to the bottom of the mug. We have brick floors and I don't want the coaster to fall and break.

These are special coasters. We bought them at Margaritaville in Orlando when we went to Universal Studios and I love these coasters. They have parrots on them and a beautiful beach scene.

One of the set of four is already broken and I don't want to break another one. I quickly put the mug and the stuck coaster back on my desk. In my haste, I spill some coffee.

I don't spill much coffee but now I am annoyed. The spill interrupts my train of thought. I immediately blame Sheri for bringing me a dirty mug. Then, I blame the kids because they didn't wash the mug thoroughly the previous day.

As I reach for the tissues to mop up the spilled coffee, I realize that if I had been more careful I would not have spilled the coffee. I start to feel guilty.

Can you relate to what I'm saying? Something happens and you feel guilty so you blame other people to ease your guilt. Then, you feel guilty for blaming the other people. It messes with your Peace of Mind.

Well, that's where I am.

The irony is that I am writing about how to have Peace of Mind when it happens. Fortunately, I immediately see that irony.

I laugh at myself. I think about what I am writing and realize that everyone has done his or her best.

Sheri wanted to please me by bringing a cup of coffee. She didn't know the mug or maybe the coaster was sticky.

Our kids do a great job washing the dishes. Maybe they missed a spot on the mug. Maybe they didn't.
I was thinking about other things when I picked up the mug. In spite of

that, I managed not to break the coaster by placing the mug on the desk before the coaster fell off the bottom of it. I really had avoided any damage.

When I realize that everyone did the best he or she could do, I feel joyful and lighthearted!

The blame goes away. The guilt goes away. I easily forgive because there is no harm.

I experience the Miracle of love.

> **Conspiracy Questions**
>
> *What do I feel guilty about today?*
>
> *Whom do I blame for my failures, pains, and discomfort?*
>
> *What fears do you have?*

Chapter 6

Love allows Miracles to take place.

Love allows shortcuts through time and space.

Molecular science appears to be Magic. We use our thoughts, words, actions, and habits to receive our Desire.

We move slowly through time and space, creeping ever so slowly toward our Desire. We learn principals of manifesting. We intend. We affirm. We practice.

As we go through this process, we experience life. We learn lessons. We grow. We love.

Then, suddenly, without warning, a Miracle takes place and we accomplish more in a day than we accomplished in the previous year.

Quantum physicists call it a quantum leap. You are at one place and suddenly, you are at another place. Normally, it would take hours or days to make that move. However, the move is instantaneous, without time advancing, and without any memory of going through space.

That is The Law of Miracles. I experience it when my life partner enters my life.

Several people could have been my choice for a partner to help me receive my Desire. I develop relationships with four wonderful people. However, for one reason or another, each of these relationships grows to a point and goes no further.

I wait. I do what I know to do. I change my thoughts, words, actions, and habits to prepare me to receive my Desire.

One of my actions is to work at two part-time jobs to make money. One job is as director of a coffeehouse. My responsibilities include playing keyboards in a music group and writing original music for songs. Sometimes I write the words and other times, they come from other people.

In the fall of 1984, I have a beautiful musical accompaniment but no

words. No one else has words either. Nothing fits the music. As fall turns into winter, a new female attendee at the coffeehouse approaches and says, "You write music don't you?"
I say "yes."

"See what you can do with this" is her reply and she hands me a sheet of lined paper with handwritten words.

I thank her and tuck away the paper. The next time I play the piano; I pull out the paper and try the new words with my new music. Amazingly, the words fit perfectly with the music. I don't have to change a syllable or a note.

As you probably guessed, the writer of these words for my music is Sheri.

We spend time together over the next few weeks polishing the song so she can sing it for a Sunday morning church service.

She becomes a friend. However, I don't consider her a romantic interest until my mother makes her "wedding" comments.

I talk with her about my Desire and she loves the idea.

Our relationship takes a quantum leap forward during that spring Sunday morning on March 31, 1985.

I finish the conversation with the voice in my head knowing that today is the day I will ask Sheri's Dad to marry her. I get out of bed. I go to church. Afterwards, I meet Sheri and her family at their house for lunch.

Sheri, her mom and her sisters prepare side dishes inside the house while I join her father, Larry, as he cooks steaks on the grill outside.

Our conversation is very one-sided as Larry drones on and about how people in the west are different from people in the east. I listen patiently but I'm puzzled about the conversation. I have what I want in North Carolina.

I have lived in Virginia and North Carolina for my entire life. I see no reason to live in the west. I have no Desire to move. The entire conversation seems pointless to me.

I can no longer stand the one-sided conversation and I try to find a way to end it. I ask a question.

"Why do you think it is so important that I know how people in the west are different from people in the east?

"Because when you marry Sheri, you will spend time in the western part of the United States."

That was obvious - just like the voice in my head said it would be. I didn't have to bring up the topic of marrying Sheri with her Dad. He starts the conversation. I am amazed.

I stutter, "M-M-Maybe we need to talk about that."

I ask permission to marry his daughter and he says it is OK with him if it is OK with her.

Later that afternoon, Sheri and I go for a walk and I ask her to marry me. She says yes.

It is a Miracle, a shortcut through time and space.

Finding a partner with the same Desire seems so difficult, until it happens. Then, a series of events, seemingly outside of my control, happen to bring about a moment where I move from being single to preparing for marriage. It is a quantum leap.

Was it outside my control? Did I really do something to cause this to happen? Was there a greater force at work?

I answer those questions in the following chapters.

> ### *Recommended Reading*
>
> *A Course in Miracles - You will not read this overnight. However, if you truly wish to understand miracles, I highly recommend this book.*

The Law of Attraction

Chapter 7

In the summer of 1984, I attend a seminar in the Baltimore, Maryland Civic Center. As I listen to the material, a Desire grows within me. It impresses me. It excites me. It emotionally charges me.

More than twenty years later, this Desire is still with me. It is a driving, compelling Desire. It is the Desire to create a family of fifty people in three generations to make the world a better place.

Step one - find a wife.

Several people could have been my choice for a partner to help me receive my Desire. I develop relationships with four wonderful people. However, for one reason or another, each of these relationships grows to a point and goes no further.

I wait. I do what I know to do. I change my thoughts, words, actions, and habits to prepare me to receive my Desire.

One of my actions is to work at two part-time jobs to make money. One job is as director of a coffeehouse. My responsibilities include playing keyboards in a music group and writing original music for songs. Sometimes I write the words and other times, the words come from other people.

In the fall of 1984, I have a beautiful musical accompaniment but no words. No one else has words either. Nothing fits the music. As fall turns into winter, a new female attendee at the coffeehouse approaches and says, "You write music don't you?"

I say "yes."

"See what you can do with this" is her reply and she hands me a sheet of lined paper with handwritten words.

I thank her and tuck away the paper. The next time I play the piano;

I pull out the paper and try the new words with my new music.

Amazingly, the words fit perfectly with the music. I don't have to change a syllable or a note.

The writer of these words for my music is a young woman named Sheri.

We spend time together over the next few weeks polishing the song so she can sing it for a Sunday morning church service.

Our relationship grows out of this time together and within three months, we recognize we share a similar Desire. We decide to spend the rest of our life together accomplishing that Desire. That is the Law of Attraction at work.

The Law of Attraction states that Attraction happens automatically through the principle of sympathetic vibration.

Science demonstrates that all items constantly vibrate. Items that appear to be solid consist of vibrating molecules. Thoughts and words vibrate. There are no proven exceptions.

These vibrations take place as waves. Waves vibrating at the same frequency are said to be "in sympathy" with one another. The term for this is "sympathetic vibration."

The root word for "sympathetic" is "sympathy." When you feel sympathy towards someone, you feel what he or she feels because the two of you vibrate at the same frequency.

This shared energy appears magical because it produces amazing results. These results include healthy relationships, beautiful music, and architectural wonders.

In addition, it is logical. It is easy to explain. It is The Law of Attraction.

The Law of Attraction has three elements. They are:

1. My Emotional Intensity Is More Important Than The Emotion
2. My Perspective Determines What I See
3. I Always Get What I Desire

> **Conspiracy Question**
>
> *When was the last time I felt what someone else felt? (Sympathy)*

Chapter 8

ELEMENT ONE: Emotional Intensity Is More Important Than The Emotion

The Law of Attraction uses emotional energy. Feelings of love, hate, passion, or anger towards something give power to that item and attract it to you.

Notice that the key is not the type of emotion. The key is the intensity of the emotion.

Love and hate both attract because both are strong emotions producing strong energy.

Any emotion - love, hate, anger, passion, fear, joy - produces energy. The more intense the feeling, the more energy produced.

The word emotion has motion in it.

Likewise, when you feel emotion, you move.

All movement consists of wave energy. The more emotion you feel, the more you move. The more waves you create. This is simple physical science applied to life.

Let's look at how this works in a personal relationship.

Before I go further, you need to understand something. You cannot manipulate other people through the Law of Attraction. You can attract certain circumstances into your life such as a committed relationship with a loving person. However, if the person you are currently with is not interested in a committed relationship with a loving person, they will be repelled from you.

The Law of Attraction does not change other people. It attracts those who Desire what you Desire and repels those who don't Desire what you Desire.

Have you ever experienced a relationship going sour? The natural reaction is to grumble and complain about it. You might even go talk to your friends about it. You focus on how bad it is.

What happens? It gets even worse. The fights intensify. The arguments increase. You grumble and complain about it to your friends. You continue focusing on how bad it is and it gets even worse!

Your emotional energy towards the negative part of the relationship actually increases the likelihood that the relationship will get worse. All your complaining and grumbling give it extra energy.

The personal relationship becomes worse as you dwell on the unpleasant parts because you empower it to do that. The result is one of two things. Either the other person stays because he wants an unpleasant relationship or the other person leaves because he does not want an unpleasant relationship.

Did you see that? Your emotional focus on the unpleasant part of the relationship either increases the intensity of the unpleasantness or drives the other person away. In fact, the only way he will stay is to fight with you. Otherwise, he is gone!

On the other hand, a pleasant personal relationship becomes better as you dwell on the pleasant parts of it. The emotions you feel empower the relationship to remain positive. If the other person wants a pleasant relationship, he stays. However, if he does not want to participate in a pleasant relationship, he leaves.

You literally attract more of what you think about because of the vibrations in your thoughts through sympathetic vibration.

Between the time I initially have my idea of a family of fifty people and the time I meet Sheri, I emit energy through thoughts and words. I write music that attracts her lyrics. She writes lyrics that attract my music. The energy created by the vibration of the piano strings radiate to her words so that by the time she gives them to me, they fit perfectly.

The Law of Attraction is strong. Sympathetic vibration is powerful.

> **Conspiracy Questions**
>
> What causes me to feel emotional?
>
> What three emotions do I feel the most often?

Chapter 9

Another term for sympathetic vibration is resonance.

I first notice the power of resonance in the early 1970s when Memorex asks the question "Is it live, or is it Memorex?" In the famous television commercials, Ella Fitzgerald sings a note that shatters a glass. Memorex records the singing onto a Memorex audio cassette. The playing back of the tape also breaks the glass.

As a kid, I thought loud volume broke the glass. I now know that it was not volume. Instead, Ella sung a note that vibrated at the same wavelength as the glass. This caused the glass to vibrate. The energy of the vibrating glass increased as Ella continued to sing until the structure of the glass shattered.

A few years later, a film shown during a high school physics class about the Tacoma Narrows Bridge gives me the next lesson on sympathetic vibration.

Architects and engineers did not fully understand sympathetic vibration when they built the Tacoma Narrows Bridge in 1940. They knew that a bridge in Manchester, England collapsed in 1831 when soldiers marched on it. The marching vibrated in resonance with the bridge and caused a wave so large that the bridge collapsed.

However, architects and engineers did not consider the effects of sympathetic vibration caused by unseen forces on a suspension bridge. As a result, sympathetic vibration caused by wind collapsed the Tacoma Narrows Suspension Bridge months after it opened.

My sympathetic vibration lessons continue during college as I earn a degree in Music Education. There, I discover that stringed instruments demonstrate sympathetic vibration.

I demonstrate this in my live presentations using a tuned guitar. I pluck the high E string - the smallest string on the guitar. Then, I put my finger against it to kill the vibration and the sound.

However, the sound continues because several other strings on the guitar vibrate from the energy produced by the high E string. The low E string plus the A and B strings produce sound even though I did not pluck them.

These examples clearly demonstrate sympathetic vibration. This phenomenon works in all parts of life. The reason is that everything contains wave energy.

The way I remember this is through the expression, "What I focus on expands." This is true even if I focus on things I do NOT like. Those things become larger and more powerful in my life because I give them extra attention.

I create energy when I focus on the things I love. I create energy when I focus on the things I hate. Either way, I create energy that sends out a wave and attracts those items to me.

Once I understand this, my next question is, "How should I respond when faced with something I dislike?"

I find the answer when I understand I do not have to oppose things I do not like. I may accept them and pass them on. I call this "remaining in the flow" and I discuss it in my writings about The Law of Abundance.

For now, let's look at how I learned this valuable information. For the first thirty-five years of my life, I study the Bible and participate in evangelical, conservative Christianity. I learn to argue moral and political issues.

When someone says something I disagree with, I argue. After all, how can I convince other people they are wrong if I don't argue with them.

What I don't know at the time is that arguing actually strengthens the opposite point of view because what I focus on expands.

My highly emotional responses of anger and extreme sadness give extra energy to the moral and political issues of the day. I join with other people who share my point of view. We give the "opposition" so much energy that we begin to see supernatural evil forces assisting our opposition.

Everyone we encounter has some kind of "demon" that we must remove through the power of Jesus. We participate in exorcisms to remove the evil spirits. We do not know that we give those spirits energy through our rabid opposition.

Our perceptions and interpretations create imaginary devils. These devils materialize and inhabit other people. It is a frightening way to live.

Then, I discover something amazing.

I learn to focus on love. I learn to focus on miracles. When I practice this, the thing I am opposing goes away. The energy is not re-enforced and it gradually dies.

When I focus on love, it expands and hate disappears. When I focus on hate, it expands and love disappears. I cannot love when I am opposing because love means acceptance.

As my understanding of The Law of Attraction grows, I understand opposition means I have an error in my perception if I want to live within The Law of Miracles and experience love.

When I do not oppose others, the vibration dies. I don't reinforce the situation through high-intensity responses. I experience Peace of Mind in relationships. I change my perception.

> ***Conspiracy Question***
>
> *What do I feel the need to fight against?*

Chapter 10

ELEMENT TWO: My Perspective Determines What I See

The past events in my life create my filter. My filter determines my current perspective.

For the first thirty-five years of my life, religion teaches me about a devil. It teaches me about an enemy.

This filter influences the way I look at everything. I see good and bad, wrong and right, God and Satan.

I see my business and the competition, my team and the opposition, my philosophy and insanity.

I do not understand that the illusion of duality happens over the truth of unity.

The reason I see so many conflicts is that I have an internal conflict between my ego, my mind, and my spirit. This conflict filters the way I see life.

I see individuals and groups fighting over religion, philosophy, morality, and politics.

This conflict creates drama that occupies much of my life. My perspective is duality and conflict.

I learn about The Law of Attraction. I recognize that the external dramas in my life come from my internal conflicts.

I begin a search to resolve the internal conflicts. I discover the source of my internal conflicts.

God programs my spirit before I am born. That is my passion, my Desire. This is my deepest, internal programming. When I live through this Desire, I am "in the flow." This Desire never leaves.

My subconscious mind understands this Desire.

When born into a body, I obtain an ego. My ego interacts with societal influences such as religion, government, and family. These influences add programming to my mind. Some of this programming supports my Desire. However, much of it does not support my Desire.

At the conscious/body/ego level, pleasing society replaces the Desire to follow my passion.

At the Desire/spirit level, the Desire to follow my passion never leaves.

At the subconscious/mind level, a conflict rages.

The conflict in my life filters how I see everything around me. I see conflict, war, and struggle.

My life reflects this struggle.

I become conscious of my Desire. However, I move slowly towards my goal because I think life is a struggle.

My perspective is duality and conflict. I learn about filters.

I discover that whenever a person responds to me, it is because of the filter on his or her life.

I discover that whether I see that response as positive or negative is because of the filter on my life.

We use filters in all parts of life.

For example, I use a filter called cable television. We have hundreds of channels that I can access at the push of a button. I don't watch a lot of television but, when I watch it, I want to select exactly what I want to see. I can select from hundreds of channels and, if there is nothing I want to watch there, I can go to the "On Demand" service to watch something archived there. There are hundreds of choices and I filter out all but one through using the remote control to select my channel.

The cable TV analogy opens my understanding of personal filters. Research shows there are thousands of messages sent to my brain every second. These include the sounds I hear, the sights I see, the odors I smell, and the feel of clothing against my skin. In addition, there is the pumping of the blood through my body and the processing of air by my lungs. My filter selects the information I need to recognize just as the remote control selects the channels on my television.

My filter determines how to interpret other people's statements and actions. I evaluate it as praise or criticism. If I determine it is praise, I feel good about myself. I associate that good feeling with the person who made the statement. I decide I like that person.

If I determine it is criticism, I feel bad about myself. I associate that bad feeling with the person who made the statement. I decide I dislike that person.

My filter determines how I interpret the other person's response. More importantly, my filter also determines how the other person responds to me.

The other person only responds to me because I attract that response. My personal resonance attracts that response.

If I feel good about what I do, I receive positive statements. If I feel bad about what I do, I receive negative statements.

If I am not sure how I feel about what I do, I receive both positive and negative statements. In addition, this means I have an internal conflict.

As I said earlier, this internal conflict rages in the mind between my spirit/Desire and my body/ ego.

Since my perspective is duality and conflict, I interpret events based on my duality and conflict filter.

Over time, I change my filter. I realize that every external conflict I experience represents my internal conflict at the time.

My perspective changes when I integrate my body/ego with my spirit/Desire.

As my filter narrows, I eliminate the illusion of duality. I see the truth of unity.

My perspective changes from duality to unity.
At this point, my entire being vibrates in sympathy with itself.

I integrate all parts of my being for one purpose. I experience "integrity."

Integrity produces the most intense personal energy. It creates peace.

This peace comes as I identify my Desire and bring my entire being into alignment with that Desire. I change my filter to create my perspective of unity.

My perspective of unity allows me to see the same thing in a different way.

I write about how I made that change in the next chapter.

> *Conspiracy Questions*
>
> *Do I primarily see life in terms of duality or unity?*
>
> *Why?*

Chapter 11

ELEMENT THREE: I Always Get What I Desire

Before birth, God programs my spirit with my Desire.

During childhood, society programs my body/ego to please others.

The conflict between my spirit and body plays out in my subconscious/mind.

Once I understand this, I decide to change perspective from duality to unity so that my entire being may resonate with my Desire. This is integrity because I integrate all parts of my being to accomplish my Desire.

Integrity has many benefits.

When I experience integrity, I can listen to my feelings and determine if what I am doing is what I want. Moving closer to my Desire resonates within my being and my joy increases. Moving away from my Desire interferes with my internal vibration and creates strife.

When I experience integrity, it is easier to build relationships because other people feel my confidence. They sense my positive vibration.

When I try to please the people around me, I am out of integrity. This confuses other people because my frequency is always changing.

This makes communication difficult at best, impossible at worst. My relationships suffer.

When I initially decide to change my perspective from duality to unity, I think the battle is between my conscious and subconscious. I spend great energy attempting to reprogram my mind.

The problem with this way of thinking is that it is still duality.

The battles still rages. I still experience conflict with those around me. I attempt to resolve this conflict.

With my perspective of duality, I see conflict and resolution as a normal part of life.

Art, literature, music, math, science, politics, and many other topics use conflict and resolution as a crucial element. At least that is my perception.

I think conflict and resolution come from change.

I'm not the only one. Much of our Western civilization believes this. I fight to maintain integrity. This struggle persists. I feel separated from my Desire.

I believe that society is conspiring against me. I talk about unity. I explain unity.

I live in duality.

Then, one quote changes my perspective.

"It may seem like luck. It is not. The truth is that life is conspiring in your favor. It may not look that way at the time. However, everything that happens brings you closer to that which you Desire."

I realize that even my opposition brings me closer to what I Desire. When I see my opposition as God's hands bringing me my Desire, my perspective changes.

I understand that my conflicts do not come from change. Change is a normal part of life.

However, I resist change because I think change requires internal conflict and resolution.

When I have internal conflict, I attract external conflicts. The only way to resolve the external conflicts is to resolve the internal ones.

I recognize that change is normal. It is healthy. It is growth. Life must have change to exist.

My conflicts come from my perspective of duality.

When I change my perspective to unity, conflict disappears. My Desire, given to me by God must come to me. God decrees it. I decree it.

The Universe works in harmony to bring it to me.

I discover that the key to receiving the maximum benefit from the Law of Attraction and receiving my Desire is changing perspective.

With the perspective of duality, everything opposes me.

With the perspective of unity, nothing opposes me. Everything works on my behalf to bring me what I Desire.

> **Conspiracy Question**
>
> *What does "Life is a Conspiracy for Me" mean to me?*
>
> *This little phrase means a great deal to me. It lifts me up when situations get me down.*
>
> *Not only do all things work together for good, all things work together by design for my benefit.*

Chapter 12

Once I discover that I can easily get what I Desire if I establish and maintain a perspective of unity, I program my subconscious for this. This is helpful.

It removes old programming and brings me closer to Desire. This enacts The Law of Attraction by using sympathetic vibration to manifest what I Desire.

My perspective of unity brings love. This enacts The Law of Miracles. The Law of Miracles allows me to experience shortcuts in time and space.

I learn that to truly experience love, I must see others as myself and myself as others.

I know that, by definition, seeing others as myself is unity.

This makes sense to me. Love is unity. Unity is love. However, this concept feels vague.

Therefore, in an attempt to identify the details of it, I list what love/unity looks like.

It means I completely trust everyone in my life.

It means God/the Universe is orchestrating events to benefit me - even the things that, at first appearance, seem to harm me.

It means I love many through the practice of Polyamory. It means I can be completely naked with everyone.

It means everything in my life moves me toward my ultimate Desire. This process works to bring Sheri and me together in 1985.

Her family moves to New Mexico in April of that year. She stays in North Carolina to finish her last semester of school and moves to New Mexico in September. Our wedding date is January 1, 1986. I fly to New Mexico for the first time on December 29.

We marry, spend our honeymoon traveling back to North Carolina, and start the next chapter of our lives together.

Our sympathetic vibration draws us to one another.

Our perspective allows us to see a future of change for the world.
We get what we Desire - or at least the beginning of it.

We establish our new perspective and discover it is challenging to maintain in our society.

We learn how to maintain it through the Law of Abundance. I write about that Law next.

> **Conspiracy Questions**
>
> *Whom do I trust the least?*
>
> *What benefit do I receive from my relationship with this person?*
>
> *Can I love this person?*
>
> *How can I demonstrate love to this person?*
>
> *What current situation harms me the most?*
>
> *What benefit do I receive from this situation?*

The Law of Abundance

Chapter 13

In the summer of 1984, I attend a seminar in the Baltimore, Maryland Civic Center. As I listen to the material, a Desire grows within me. It impresses me. It excites me. It emotionally charges me.

More than twenty years later, this Desire is still with me. It is a driving, compelling Desire. It is the Desire of creating a family of fifty people in three generations to make the world a better place.

I meet my future wife, Sheri, in the fall of 1984. She has a similar Desire and decides to join me during the spring of 1985. We marry on January 1, 1986.

With step one accomplished, we move to step two - have children. Since our goal is to have eight children, we determine that time is of the essence and we do what newlyweds do. We start the reproduction process.

We expect to have our first child by our first anniversary. Two months go by and Sheri is not pregnant. Two months become five, and five months become seven.

We wonder if we're doing it right. We hear stories of couples becoming pregnant while using birth control. We aren't using birth control and we aren't pregnant. We won't have a child by our first anniversary.

However, on August 1, after seven full months of marriage, Sheri discovers she is pregnant. We are thrilled beyond measure. We are on our way.

By November, the doctors think something is amiss and they schedule an ultrasound for Thanksgiving week. My parents are visiting for the holiday and they join us at the doctor's office.

There is tension in the room as the doctor starts the procedure by putting gel on Sheri's stomach. The gel is a conductor for sound waves.

Next, he uses a transducer to send sound waves into the uterus. The sound waves bounce off bones and tissue returning back to the transducer to generate black and white images. We are using technology to see inside Sheri's body.

The doctor looks on the screen to confirm his suspicions. We look with him as he explains carefully what we see. He points to something on the right side of Sheri's abdomen and says, "There is the baby."

Then, he points to something on the left side of her abdomen and says, "There is the other baby."

We are having twins. Both babies are healthy and normal. We celebrate Thanksgiving with tremendous enthusiasm.

I didn't have a name for it at the time but we were experiencing something profound. It was the Law of Abundance at work.

The Law of Abundance states everything reproduces through multiplication over time to produce resources sufficient for all Desire.

Some people believe in the Law of Abundance. Others believe in scarcity or lack.

When I first share my vision of creating a family of fifty people in three generations to make a positive impact the world, I discover that most of my friends believe in scarcity.

They oppose my abundant vision. They doubt me when I talk about it. When Sheri and I marry, they take me aside and say it is unfair to ask her to have eight children.

Then, they said we cannot afford to have eight children and teach them at home.

On the other hand, a few of my friends believe in abundance.

They see the demonstrations of this law in our daily lives. They understand that lack is always temporary and that nature is infinitely abundant.

Their abundant attitudes encourage us as we start towards the fulfillment of our vision. Their generosity paves the way for us to take the next step.

There are three elements in The Law of Abundance. They are:

1. Abundance is a Normal Act of Nature
2. Lack is Always Temporary
3. Gratefulness Accelerates the Law of Abundance

> **Conspiracy Questions**
>
> *Do I believe in lack or abundance? Why?*

Chapter 14

ELEMENT ONE: Abundance is a Normal Act of Nature

The design of nature is reproduction through multiplication. One seed of corn planted, grown, and cared for produces an infinite amount of corn.

This is true throughout nature. Let's look at some example from the Southwestern United States.

Tumbleweeds are a huge part of the Southwestern landscape. We have so many in New Mexico that we make snowmen out of them during the holiday season.

Did you know that real name of the plant is "Russian Thistle" and that tumbleweed did not appear in the United States until 1877?

The first recorded tumbleweed was in South Dakota in 1877. By 1900, tumbleweed spread to the Pacific coast.

It is so abundant today that most people think it has always been part of our Western landscape.

There are no limits to the number of offspring produced by anything in nature.

Our family lives in a high mountain desert valley. There are examples of abundance all around us. The juniper trees and cactus grow easily. We see flowering plants every spring, summer, and fall. The birds and wildlife are everywhere.

As I write this material, I only have to turn my head and look out the window to see an assortment of doves, finches, towhees, blue jays, and sparrows. By the time each day is over, I see rabbits, quail, crows, vultures, hawks and a surprise or two like a cedar waxwing, grosbeak, or red-winged blackbird. During the summer, more than fifty hummingbirds visit our feeders daily.

Abundance is strong and vibrant in nature. It overcomes many obstacles.

How to Have and Maintain Peace of Mind

We live on a rural road. It was a dirt road until just a few years ago. Then, the county covered the dirt with asphalt. A few months after the asphalt project was completed, we took an evening walk.

Imagine our surprise when we noticed plants growing through the asphalt. That's right, the asphalt had been laid down and compressed on top of those plants but that didn't stop them. They grew right through it. That is the Law of Abundance at work.

The valley we live in is located east of the Sandia Mountains. These mountains are a study in contrasts. The reasons for the contrasts are climatic. The winds are normally from the west. The west side of the Sandias receives the brunt of those winds. They serve as a counter measure against any moisture that may wander into the area. After the winds hit the west side of the mountain, they go up and over the mountain to blow across the plains of eastern New Mexico. The mountain protects our little valley from the strongest winds.

When cooler Canadian air comes into the area from the north, it moves down the east side of the Sandias. The mountain range traps it there. This cooler air wrings out any moisture coming over the mountain. If the Canadian cold front is especially strong, it will hold the moisture against the mountain for a day or two but not push the moisture over the mountain. As a result, the east side of the mountains receives twice the rainfall as the west side.

I have lived in that valley over twenty years and I'm amazed at how the mountain is so different on one side than the other.

The west side of the mountain is pure desert with sparse vegetation. The east side of the mountain is a national forest.

There is a beautiful drive through the national forest on the east side. I have taken it many times. The juniper and ponderosa give way to the spruce trees that give way to the aspens. The environment changes at the end of the drive on the top of the mountain. The trees give way to rocks and sheer cliffs. However, abundance exists on the west side of the mountain too!

The top part of the west side of the mountain has funny looking trees. They lean towards the east. The prevailing winds are so consistent and strong that the trees are not able to grow straight. The winds push them at an angle. These trees grow out of solid rock in the midst of consistent wind.

These trees face tremendous obstacles in this harsh environment. The wind batters them. The sun bakes them. The rain avoids them. Still, they manage to live. The Law of Abundance mandates that they thrive.

Of course, if you look closely around these larger trees, you will observe other, baby trees, making their way out of the rocks. They serve as an example of how nature reproduces through multiplication.

Sheri and I observe this in our lives also. Nineteen months after the twins' birth, we add a baby girl to our family, and then, every other year for the next ten years, we add another child. The Law of Abundance allows us to reproduce through multiplication.

Examples of the Law of Abundance are everywhere. If you live in an urban environment, thank the Law of Abundance the next time you wait in line at the grocery or you become stuck in a traffic jam. The Law of Abundance is a universal principle.

Drive around in the poorest neighborhoods and look at the abundance. Notice the collection of possessions. The possessions may not be your choice of possessions but they are abundant. They could be broken down cars, dogs on a porch, or a plethora of plastic pink flamingos. Whatever you see, I promise you it will be a demonstration of abundance.

Look around where you live. Do you have enough room to store everything you have? Are closets and garages jammed full of abundance? Do you have enough time in the day to do what you want to do? Is your day crammed with an abundance of activities? As you can see, abundance naturally happens everywhere.

Of course, that leaves the question. If the Law of Abundance is true, then why do we sometimes observe lack or feel like we don't have enough?

> **Conspiracy Question**
>
> *What evidence of reproduction through multiplication do I see?*

Chapter 15

ELEMENT TWO: Lack is Always Temporary

Once I learn that abundance always happens. I have to ask the question, "Why do I sometimes see lack?"

For example, a fire wipes out a forest leaving a barren wasteland that appears void of life. The same fire escapes the forest and moves into a residential area destroying homes and possessions. The owners of those items experience lack.

Or, in another example, a hurricane produces a flood that devastates a coastal environment. The flood overruns levees and other barriers. It destroys residential and commercial structures. The owners of these properties experience lack.

As I think about it, I realize that, in each case, the lack is temporary. The remnants of the fire produce an environment that allows life to rejuvenate quickly. The flood scrubs and cleans the coastal area of pollutants so that life can thrive in an unprecedented manner.

The property owners in these areas rebuild completely or move to a different area where they may experience abundance.

These natural "disaster" examples demonstrate the Law of Abundance at work to create increased resources through first creating temporary lack. They teach a valuable lesson.

Let's look closer.

The elements of nature, (wind, water, earth, and fire) function through movement. If something blocks that movement, lack occurs.

A dammed river produces a lake above the dam. Downstream, areas that once benefitted from the water now turn brown.

However, the movement continues. The blockage cannot remain in place forever. It must eventually yield to the movement or break.

A dam must release water periodically or it will break.

The buildup and release of pressure occurs throughout nature and throughout life.

The size of the buildup determines the violence of the release. Nature removes brush buildup with fire.

For years, the United States National Park Service saw fire as an enemy. When a fire started, they put it out immediately. After doing this for decades, they realized that some of the fires were so large they couldn't control them.

The reason is that fire is part of the flow of nature. If man doesn't interfere, the forests self-maintain themselves and a fire burns for hours or days. If man interferes, the resulting fires are so big they burn for weeks or months. The forests maintain themselves either way. They can do so gently or with great violence.

The size of the brush determines the violence of the fire.

Other natural examples of buildup and release include earthquakes and weather storms.

When this buildup happens in a person's body, the results include heart attacks, constipation, strokes, and acne. Sometimes great force such as surgery and other invasive treatments must release the blockage. Meanwhile, exercise, peaceful thinking, and proper diet keep the body's systems flowing and prevent these symptoms.

Violent releases often produce dramatic results. In nature, violent releases produced some of the United States National Parks including Grand Canyon, Zion Canyon, Yellowstone, and Yosemite.

The lesson I learn is that The Law of Abundance always works. When The Law of Abundance flows, life is gentle. When The Law of Abundance is blocked, there is temporary lack until release happens in a dramatic and often violent breakthrough.

I decide I want a gentle life, a life of peace and happiness.

In my search for peace, I realize that unity brings love and love brings peace.

I realize that lack is a perspective of duality.

When I have a perspective of unity, the destructive fire that causes lack is an abundance of fire. The raging storm that destroys property is an abundance of wind and water.

Abundance always produces abundance. There is no such thing as permanent lack.

When I have a perspective of duality, I see lack.

My perspective of lack is a warning. It is a red flag.

Lack is an indicator that my perspective has shifted from unity to duality.

Once I realize this, I discover there are other red flags that indicate I am looking at something from the perspective of duality instead of my Desired perspective of unity.

> *Conspiracy Question*
>
> *What do I lack?*

Chapter 16

Living with Peace of Mind means that I choose to live from a perspective of unity rather than a perspective of duality.

This perspective allows me to love all. It allows me to pursue my Desire. It allows me to experience the free flow of miracles into my life.

However, because our society usually sees things through a perspective of duality, I find it easy and natural to move back to a perspective of duality.

Elections, religions, sports, and business appear to consist of "us versus them."

The world appears to operate based on hot/cold, white/black, rich/poor, and right/wrong.

A perspective of duality is easy to believe. It causes guilt, blame, and fear.

I once believed in duality so much that I thought conflict and resolution were the basis of life.

A perspective of duality is addictive.

Duality is the basis of drama. The emotion that goes with drama creates adrenaline and produces a physical high.

I was so addicted to the high caused by drama that if my life did not contain drama, I created it.

I lived a life based on guilt, blame, and fear. If I was not experiencing the high from guilt, blame, and fear, I created situations that brought those things to me.

Once I become convinced that changing perspective from duality to unity is a worthy goal, I discover obstacles to the change. All of these obstacles are thoughts I have learned over my life. They are techniques I learned to survive in a world of duality.

The obstacles are easy to change when I realize what they are. My Desire to love others allows me to experience The Law of Miracles. I break old habits and form new ones in a matter of days or hours rather than taking the three to four weeks usually accustomed with new habits.

However, some of these obstacles are subtle.

Guilt feels like humility and gives me an excuse not to love myself so I can better love others.

Blame allows me to love myself because other people do the same thing so I think I'm not so bad.

Fear feels like love because I'm protecting myself and others from outside dangers.

Guilt, blame, and fear disguise themselves as love so I have trouble recognizing them.

Therefore, I need clues to see guilt, blame, and fear. I call those clues "red flags" because they are warnings that something needs attention. They tell me that I'm looking at something from the perspective of duality.

They tell me that the love I think I am feeling is really guilt, blame, or fear.

Here is the list of red flags. Memorize it and you are on your way to a perspective of unity.

   1. Resistance

That's it. Resistance

Whenever I'm resistant to anything that happens in my life, I'm out of the flow. I'm operating from a perspective of duality rather than a perspective of unity. I'm blocking my ability to recognize The Law of Abundance.

A red flag means guilt, blame, or fear exists. However, I don't feel guilt, blame, or fear. I feel love to some and resistance to others.

I have learned that every time I feel resistance, there is underlying guilt, blame, or fear causing that resistance.

Resistance is THE red flag. Let's look closer at resistance.

Resisting anything in my life is like driving a sports car as fast as I can with my foot on the brake. It is violent, loud, and unproductive.

When something arrives into my life, it is too late to change it. It is too late to do anything about it. I can only accept it and respond. I cannot change it.

When I complain and resist, I become like that sports car. I am violent, loud, and unproductive.

If I believe in The Law of Attraction, I attract everything into my life. If I attract a challenge into my life, I attracted it to spotlight an area of resistance that I need to remove. It really is that simple.

If I feel like hiding, I'm resisting what I have attracted into my life. I feel guilty.

If I feel hurt, I'm resisting the good that I can receive from the situation. I am blaming the situation.

If I see an opponent, I'm resisting the help that comes from his influence. I am blaming another person.

If I see lack, I'm resisting the truth of abundance. I'm afraid there isn't enough.

During our first year of marriage, Sheri and I have a perspective of duality. We see lack.

We think we will have a child during our first year of marriage. We do not.

Because we live within the dimension of time, Sheri and I use time to measure the speed of The Law of Abundance. While waiting to become pregnant with our first child, we think the process is taking too long.

This thought comes from a perspective of lack, a perspective of duality. This perspective says, "If you have something, I cannot have it." It is the basis of war and conflict.

We don't have one child after one year. For the first seven months of our marriage, until Sheri becomes pregnant, we experience what we think is lack.

However, we're in the perfect situation to learn about abundance. We have a large house to live in during the first 14 months of our marriage. It has six bedrooms and four bathrooms. It is an abundant house for newlyweds.

During that time, we offer a room to a local pregnancy center. One of their clients, a single, expectant mother, stays with us. Sheri learns about the pregnancy experience and is present when our houseguest gives birth.
In addition, a neighbor's cat decides to birth her kittens on our front porch. Sheri helps with the delivery.

These two experiences increase her understanding of pregnancy and delivery. This changes her perspective.

We begin to see abundance.

Then, Sheri becomes pregnant. We discover we're having twins, and we have two children after fourteen months instead of one child after twelve.

We experience a miracle, a shortcut in time and space. We experience abundance. This perspective says, "There is more than enough for everybody." It is the basis of peace.

Notice that our perspective of duality did not prevent The Law of Abundance from working. The law is always working. The perspective of duality only prevents recognition of The Law of Abundance.

With the perspective of duality, the new asphalt on our road slows down the growth of the plants underneath.

With the perspective of duality, a fire destroys trees.

With the perspective of duality, a flood wipes out a nesting area for wildlife.

With the perspective of duality, Sheri and I think we may never have children.

With the perspective of unity, the plants benefit from the asphalt and grow through it.

With the perspective of unity, the fire creates the perfect environment for the seeds left behind to quickly germinate and create more trees.

With the perspective of unity, the flood leaves behind a clean area with greater capability for reproduction.

With the perspective of unity, Sheri and I realize that abundance is a normal act of nature and lack is always temporary.

The Law of Abundance is natural. It is life. It is always there. However, we often don't see it because of our perspective. We don't see it because we have blocked our view with resistance.

> **Conspiracy Question**
>
> *What am I resistant to in my life today?*

Chapter 17

ELEMENT THREE: Gratefulness and The Law of Abundance.

This element is where all of the Laws of the Southwest Lifestylecome together.

Let's review.

The Law of Miracles works through understanding my Desire and using thoughts, words, actions, and habits to learn how to love.

Guilt, blame, and fear resist love and temporarily block the flow of miracles to me.

The Law of Attraction works with my emotional focus. When I am single-minded, the emotional intensity creates powerful waves that attract anything else vibrating at that frequency.

When I am confused, I emit two or more different frequencies. This prevents the intensity because the waves interfere with one another. My confusion temporarily blocks what I want to attract.

I cooperate with The Law of Miracles when I learn how to love. I cooperate with The Law of Attraction when I have a singular emotional focus.

I cooperate with The Law of Abundance when I express gratefulness.

The most powerful way to express gratefulness is through acts of generosity.

The emotion of gratefulness expressed through acts of generosity releases The Law of Abundance in my life.

Generosity is the human equivalent of the flow of nature that is necessary for water, fire, wind, and earth to function.

Without generosity, I create resistance and block the flow of The Law of Abundance.

Let's use the science of vibration to see how this works.

When a possession arrives into my life, I respond in one of three ways.

1. I accept it and share it.
2. I accept it and keep it.
3. I resist it.

These physical acts of sharing, keeping, and resisting have an associated energy.

Since everything is energy and energy travels in waves, the science of vibration explains what happens to my energy when I share, keep, or resist.

SHARING

When a wave travels through space, it gradually loses energy. When I accept something and share it, I add energy to the wave so it can go on to others and bless them.

Generosity accepts the energy and transmits it on so that I experience abundance. In fact, when I give generously, I add energy to what I receive so that the wave goes further.

This is the explanation behind the expression, "Money likes action." Money is a form of energy. When I act, I receive energy, I pass it on, and I experience the benefits. The more I act, the more energy I receive, the more energy I have to pass on and the more benefits I experience.

Action removes things from my life and replaces them with other things. This quick movement attracts more energy. The energy flies into my hands. If I pass it along, I receive the benefits.

When I have too many things, obstacles appear in the form of clutter. These obstacles block the energy. I can only maintain responsibility for so many possessions. When too many items accumulate, there is nowhere to put any new items.

The Law of Abundance continues to work. Possessions continue to come. They gradually weigh me down until I am not able to move.

They create a bottleneck.

At this point, delegation becomes a priority. I have to give things away. Sometimes, I give away responsibilities. Sometimes, I give away possessions. Sometimes, I give away money. In every case, I give away the energy I receive so I may receive more.

KEEPING

When a wave travels through space and encounters "soft" or absorbent material, the wave transfers energy to the material and dies.

When I keep something, I take all the energy from the wave. I block the flow with things I already have.

My hoarding, caused by a fear of lack, kills the energy and prevents me from experiencing abundance. When I keep something, I stagnate. More energy attempts to come to me. However, I cannot receive it because I only have so much capacity.

When a dam blocks a river, there has to be spillways and other methods of allowing the water to go downstream. Otherwise, the water will overflow the dam or the dam will break and cause great destruction.

Likewise, I must have releases in my life. Otherwise, when I reach my capacity, the next inflow of energy causes me to overflow. The release of this overflow of energy is usually destructive.

RESISTING

When a wave travels through space and meets resistance, the wave receives energy to go back in the opposite direction. If the wave source still exists, this amplifies the wave and causes it to grow larger.

When I resist something, I do not kill the wave. I add energy to the wave. This creates conflict and produces guilt and blame.

This resistance prevents me from experiencing other blessings that may come into my life because I cannot accept and resist at the same time.

In addition, I fail at my resistance because anything that comes into my life is there because The Law of Attraction brings it to me.

Once it arrives, I can only try to resist it. However, I can never permanently resist it.

The reason is that it is impossible to accept and resist at the same time. Those two actions are out of integrity with each other. When I resist what comes into my life, I deny reality. The more I resist it, the more it remains.

Whenever I give something attention, it remains. What I resist persists.

It may appear to leave but it doesn't. If it is in my life, I attracted it to myself. The Law of Attraction brought it to me. If I resist it, it will come back stronger the next time. The reason is that I am giving it more attention. I strengthen the energy by resisting it.

Mother Theresa was a woman of peace but she would not attend an anti-war rally. She only attended peace rallies. She understood that resisting something only gives it more energy.

When what I initially resist comes back to me, it is stronger and bigger than before.

I may resist it once, twice, or more and it will continue to come back until it is so big it overwhelms me. At that point, it may be destructive.

Whereas, when I accept it and pass it on the first time it arrives, I experience Peace of Mind because I allow it to flow instead of blocking it.

This is true with every energy form. Water, wind, earth, fire, money, and love work this way.

My gratefulness, even in the face of difficulty, allows me to learn and grow. I then may take that lesson and generously pass it on to others.

Conspiracy Question

What clutters my life?

Chapter 18

I receive Peace of Mind when I express gratefulness through acts of generosity.

I give things away. I pass along everything I can. This is not just giving away items mindlessly. It is the wise acquiring and stewarding of possessions.

Often, there is resistance to giving. I am afraid I will need what I give away. I feel guilty that I'm giving a used item. I blame others for their negative responses to my gift.

The culprits of guilt, blame, and fear show up again and provide resistance. However, when I love, truly love, the guilt, blame, and fear disappear. When I give, I invest into other's Desire. This makes it possible for abundance to flow freely.

In addition, when I give things away, I receive a side benefit. Many of the items I give away are distractions to me. With these distractions out of the way, I am able to focus on my passion.

Without these distractions, I have an abundance of time to enjoy my Desire because I have filtered out the things I don't Desire. I become an expert on my passion. Expertise leads to wealth.

My generosity demonstrates that I have enough. Nobody can steal from me when I'm giving because when someone takes without permission, my attitude of generosity opens the channel wider so The Law of Abundance may replace those items with something better.

If I haven't used something in six months, I give it away. I can always acquire a new item.

When I discover I need something I have given away, I am able to acquire a new item that serves me better. In some cases, people offer me what I need without me having to buy it.

Generous actions reinforce my thoughts and words of gratefulness and open the channel for greater things to come my way.

I habitually look for things to remove from our life. I may sell these items. I may give them away. I may trade for something else. I may throw them away. By doing this, I experience the freedom to see the miracles my heart Desire.

All spiritual teachers emphasize the importance of generosity. They call it tithes. They call it offerings. They call it love gifts. These teachers understand that the emotion of gratefulness expressed in acts of generosity clears the bottleneck in our lives so we can receive new things.

Businesses thrive when they demonstrate generosity. They receive free publicity. They generate good will. Everyone wins in this process.

The Law of Abundance always rewards systems that generate and disperse funds. These systems move the funds without hoarding them.

John Rockefeller, Senior had a net worth of 1.7 billion dollars when he died in spite of giving away 1.3 billion dollars during his lifetime. He developed an entire organization to give away his money.

Bill Gates built great wealth at Microsoft and invested much of that wealth into a foundation. Warren Buffet, one of the wealthiest men of our generation gave most of his wealth to Bill Gates Foundation. Even with their outrageous generosity, they remain wealthy.

In fact, if you study the lives of wealthy men and women, you will notice an attitude of gratefulness demonstrated by generosity. In all cases, their generosity started before they became wealthy!!

They discovered the key to The Law of Abundance and practiced it in their lives.

My gratefulness in discovering these Law of the Southwest Lifestyle causes my Desire to share it with you so you may experience the same abundance.

If I don't share, I'm not grateful. If I love what I have, I Desire you to have it.

I Desire for you to experience the same freedoms, joy, and thrills that I have experienced.

That is why I share the Laws of the Southwest Lifestyle. Sharing is the demonstration of the Law of Abundance.

Through sharing, The Law of Abundance provides the fulfillment of my Desire.

Through sharing, The Law of Attraction attracts the sharing that I need.

Through sharing, The Law of Miracles gives me shortcuts in time and space.

I experience all of these laws in my life as I move closer to the fulfillment of my Desire.

That Desire is the one I recognize in the summer of 1984 while attending a seminar in the Baltimore Civic Center. It is the Desire to create a family of fifty people in three generations to make the world a better place.

That fall, I meet a young woman, Sheri. She has a similar Desire and we marry on January 1, 1986.

We add details to our Desire. We decide to have eight children. We decide to be debt free, including our mortgage. We decide to teach our kids at home. That means at least one of us has to work at home.

Almost twelve years later, on a brisk sunny day in the fall of 1997, I write the check for final payment on our mortgage and heave a huge sigh of relief. We are finally debt free. We have no credit card debt, no car payments, and no house payments.

We become debt free while raising seven children and educating them at home. On the day I write that final mortgage check, I feel good about life. We are on our way to fulfilling our Desire.

A little later in that same day, Sheri comes into our home office with a look on her face I have seen several other times. I raise my eyebrows and she nods. We are expecting our eighth child! What an amazing day! Two of our Desires become reality on the same day.

During the next ten years, our eighth child is born, we build our dream house, one of our daughters marries, and we become grandparents.

Through these experiences, we search for the major impact we can make on the world. We want to make the world a better place.

We identify The Laws of the Southwest Lifestyle. We write. We do what we know to do.

During our writing, our learning, our growing, we clarify our Desire. It is not eight just children. It is not merely fifty people in three generations. Those are wonderful experiences. However, they are not our deepest Desire.

Through these experiences, we realize that our Desire is to demonstrate How to Have Peace of Mind. We realize that experiencing what we call the Southwest Lifestyle is a way to do this.

We decide to put together the information in the clearest, simplest way we can so that we may share it with others.

We call this material Living the Southwest Lifestyle.

> *Conspiracy Questions*
>
> *How can I immediately demonstrate gratefulness through an act of generosity?*
>
> *What can I share today?*

Chapter 19

The Miracle of A Hidden Car

The parking lot of the Tijeras Library serves many needs. A park, a middle school and an elementary school are nearby so the library's parking lot is a meeting place for parents and kids.

In addition, local residents use the location as a coordination point for car pooling the ten miles into Albuquerque.

Of course, many people use the lot to park while using the library's reading material. I use it to park while I pick up and drop off books. That's my intent on this bright sunny fall afternoon.

As I pull into the lot, I almost notice a mom and a couple of kids scattered throughout the grassy median between the two sections of the lot. They might be looking for a lost item.

I'm in a hurry to drop off my old book and pick up a new one so the trio is background noise to me.

I get out of the truck and step over a toy car in the grass. It's a Hot Wheel or maybe a Matchbox car. I step over it and think of Isaiah, my grandson. At the young age of 18 months, he already loves these little cars. Girls love dolls and boys love cars even when they haven't had enough social programming to consciously understand their roles.

I decide to pick it up on the way back to my truck if it is still there. "If it is still there?" I think. "Why wouldn't it be there? It hides in the grass. No one will find this lost car. It is mine."

Suddenly, I hear myself say, "Hey, what are you looking for?"

I say it to one of the kids in the grass. I feel silly. He isn't obviously looking for anything.

"Huh?"

"Are you looking for a little car?"

I hold up my fingers, three inches apart to show the size. "Yeah."

Confusion reigns on his face. He can't figure out how I know about his lost car.

"It's over there"

I point to the spot. He just looks at me.

I can read his mind. "Is this an elaborate joke? Is this man picking on me? How could he know about my car? How did he know I was searching? Is this for real?"

I retrace three steps, pick up the car, and hand it to him. "Thank you."

"Sure."

I have looming appointments so I move to drop off my old book and pick up my new one. I quickly walk towards the library.

"Hey, I found it – he helped me find it."

I start up the library stairs almost unaware of what just happened. I think about it and wonder if it happened at all. I look over my shoulder to make sure I didn't dream it. The mother looks at me. She's smiling. "THANK YOU!"

"You're welcome."

It happened. For a brief few seconds, I was in the moment and the result, as always, was a miracle.

Personal Peace of Mind

How to Live Within
The Law of Miracles

Chapter 20

This Sunday morning in August 2007, a week before my oldest daughter's wedding, starts normally for me.

I quit going to organized church several years ago. However, I still have a Sunday morning routine.

I spend the first hour with my wife and our eight kids sharing what we learned during the week. Then, I watch a little ESPN while eating breakfast, followed by several hours immersed in whatever book I am reading.

This Sunday is no different from usual. However, before it is over, it is to be vastly different from any Sunday I have previously experienced.

My current reading material is Shirley MacLaine's *Dancing in the Light*. I am anxious to read the third section because the setting is Santa Fe, New Mexico, a short, 45-minute drive from my home. I sense something spectacular is about to take place in her book and in my life.

I read about her visits to a physic in Galisteo, a little community halfway between my home and Santa Fe. Her experiences put her in touch with her Higher Self (you may call that God, the Universe, or Higher Power). She receives guidance and insight into her life.

I finish the book and discover I have time to meditate. My favorite place to meditate is our hot tub so I head to the sunroom.

I get into the hot tub, sit down, and close my eyes. My meditation times are always full of insight. Most people have trouble "hearing from God."

I believe God will always speak to me if I am quiet. I simply listen, ask questions, and receive answers. It is as normal as talking to any other being. I understand that is not everybody's experience. However, it is mine.

When I close my eyes this time, I see a being that is similar in appearance to what Shirley describes in her book as her Higher Self. I have learned not to question what I see during my meditation. I just observe. I know this time is going to be significant so I focus on the message and listen closely.

The message is full of rich insights on health, relationships, and business. This being speaks to me for the next hour as I finish my time in the hot tub, move outside to bask in the noonday sun, shower, and prepare for our afternoon basketball games. It is quite remarkable.

Much of the material I receive is more appropriate for another time. However, one topic has special significance because of my daughter's upcoming wedding.

I am an only child. I grew up in Collinsville, Virginia and moved out of the house when I was 18 to attend East Carolina University. I finished my degree and remained in Greenville, North Carolina to work. I met my wife, Sheri, a couple of years later. Her family moved to New Mexico during our engagement and we were married there. My parents didn't attend the wedding.

Sheri and I lived in North Carolina for the first sixteen months of our marriage. Then, we moved to New Mexico. My parents were OK with me living four hours away but the move to New Mexico crushed them.

I didn't understand it. A part of me always thought that they released me when they didn't attend my wedding. I was never angry with them for that. It was just a symbol that they really didn't feel a need to be involved in my life at an intimate level. I accepted it and went forward.

However, I think our move caused them to recognize the significance of what they communicated through their absence. I believe Divine Providence orchestrated those events.

Now, with my daughter's wedding looming on the horizon, Mom and Dad have a decision to make. Will they come to the wedding?

The answer is obvious to me. My parents have a strong sense of fairness that will not allow them to attend. If they didn't attend their son's wedding in New Mexico, it wouldn't be fair to me for them to attend their granddaughter's wedding in New Mexico either. I know they won't be here.

I talk with my parents every Saturday morning for an hour. Sometimes there isn't much to say. Dad is not much of a talker and Mom talks about relatives, her friends, and the weather.

I tell them about my week and keep them up to date on the grandkids. We tell each other "I love you." at the end of the call and we've paid our dues for the week.
It isn't perfect but it is better than some families who never talk, so I am content with it.

Recently, the weekly calls have taken on a different air. The first question we ask is "How are you?" During the past several months, Mom's answers evolved from "I'm tired." to "I don't feel well." to "I went to the doctor/emergency room/specialist several times this week."

As I meditate on this Sunday, the voice speaks to me very clearly. "Don't be surprised if your Mother dies before the wedding Saturday."

Conspiracy Question

Would I consider this to be a Miracle?

Chapter 21

How would you respond if this happened to you?

You can imagine the doubts that could have gone through my head as I listened to the message on that Sunday in August 2007.

You may find it hard to believe that I had no doubts that day. The reason is that I believe in The Law of Miracles.

I now have a wonderful system for receiving information during meditation. However, it wasn't always that way.

I grew up in a belief system that taught good versus evil. I learned the importance of discerning right from wrong.

I was afraid of hearing from the wrong voice so I compared what I heard in my heart to the Bible. I compared it to other messages from the Divine.

I even went so far as to believe and teach that God primarily uses my authorities to speak to me.

It is the ultimate patriarchal system.

If you are an American, you are familiar with it. Those in power control others.

You may immediately think of the government, religious, and business leaders. However, it goes further than that.

Doctors, lawyers, and media members often use their positions to control others too.

This system is so prevalent that most of us accept it without a second thought.

I believed in that system. Therefore, I learned not to think for myself on important matters. I trusted the authority figures in my life.

As a result, I didn't develop a strong relationship with my Internal Source, God, or the Universe. I floundered.

If you are floundering in your life, there is only one reason. You don't know what your Life Purpose is. By the time you finish this book, you may not know your Life Purpose. However, you will know how to identify it using The Law of Miracles.

Even though my connection with the Divine was limited, I discovered my Life Purpose in 1984, as I participated in a seminar in the Baltimore, Maryland Civic Center.

More than twenty years later, this Desire is still with me. It is a driving, compelling Desire. It is the Desire of creating a family of fifty people in three generations to make the world a better place by demonstrating how to have and maintain Peace of Mind.

Even though I wasn't directly connected to my source, the message still got through to me.

Unfortunately, my religion taught that Desire is sinful or selfish. This internal philosophy allowed doubts to challenge my Life Purpose. I had internal self-talk that distracted me. That self-talk said, "the reason you want to have eight kids is so you can have unrestricted sex and not worry about birth control."

Fortunately, the authority figures in my life agreed with my Major Desire so I was comfortable moving forward with it.

However, on a larger scale, I still had a conflict between my Desire and my religion's teaching that I can't trust my Desire because it might be sinful.

Resolution came to this conflict when I learned the truth that the word "Desire" comes from the Latin word meaning "of the Father." If I have a Desire, my God put that Desire into me. It is sacred. It is holy. It is trustworthy.

Desire comes from my heart. It is eternal. It is peaceful.

I somehow knew that in 1984. I'm grateful for that knowledge. Since then, I've discovered a foolproof way to find and fulfill my Desire. It is simple.

I will briefly explain that way here. Later in this book, I will give you the opportunity to explore using this method.

I know that a Desire may be my Life Purpose or it may be a stepping-stone to get to my Life Purpose. Either way, it is there because I need to fulfill it to experience the design for my life.

For the purposes of this book, I describe two levels of Desires. The first is "Major Desire" or "Life Purpose."

The second is "mini-Desire" or a "like". I need it to fulfill my Life Purpose.

To start finding my Life Purpose, I forget about anything that resists my Desire and identify everything I like to do.

I don't judge the activities; I just identify them and write them on a list.

Here is my list of likes:

- Music
- Basketball
- Writing
- Sex
- Teaching
- TV
- Computers
- Radio
- Creative thinking
- Comedy
- Meditation
- Math/accounting/finances
- Working out
- Games
- Conversation
- Puzzles

Can you see how the Desire I found in 1984 resonated within me? I already like to do certain things.

Then - BAM - I experience a quantum leap. I suddenly have my Life Purpose in front of me and I know it is my Life Purpose because it coincides with my likes.

Those likes make it easier for me to lead a large family successfully.

I now believe that is enough to determine my life purpose. However, there were other elements to consider when looking at Life Purpose.

The Life Purpose I received in 1984 fit within my personal belief system.

In addition, the authorities in my life support my Desire. I use them as intermediaries to confirm my Desire.

I now believe that I can go directly to the Source to hear from God. However, until I became confident in that, it was important to have other people as intermediaries.

Intermediaries include Jesus, Mary, the Church, pastors, rabbis, Fathers, bosses, Lords, tarot card readers, palm readers, mediums, channels, fortunetellers, Mohammad, Moses, etc.

Since I didn't trust my ability to contact my Source directly, some of these beings and institutions played excessively prominent roles in my life.

The only reason I didn't trust my ability to contact my source is that I had been taught to not trust my likes. My religion called them lusts, sins of the flesh, and temptations.

I don't see my likes that way anymore. I use a different word for those terms.

When I write this word, I use a capital letter at the beginning to remind me it is sacred, it is holy....

That word is Desire.

Every Desire I have is holy. It is sacred. It is of the Father - even the little Desires.

Every Desire may be trusted because it comes directly from God. One of my goals with this material is to help you reconnect to the Divine part of you, just as I learned to reconnect with the Divine part of me.

When you reconnect, it is easy to identify your Desire. Remember what I said earlier about Desire.

Some religions teach that Desire might be bad. Others say that Desire is sinful or selfish.

The truth is "Desire" comes from the Latin word meaning "of the Father." If you have a Desire, your God put that Desire into you. It is sacred. It is holy. It is trustworthy.

A Desire comes from your heart. It is eternal. It is peaceful.

However, even after you learn to trust your Desire, you may want to use an intermediary at times in the relationship with your God. I think it is OK to do so.

I write about how one of my sons uses intermediaries in a practical way starting on the next Chapter.

Conspiracy Question

What is my Desire or Life Purpose?

Chapter 22

It is a sunny day in December 2005. I have worked at my desk since early morning.

Now as the clock approaches noon, my phone rings. The caller ID tells me the call is from my real estate business partner. I answer the phone, expecting to discuss a routine business matter.

"Hello, Joe."

"Matt, the house is on fire!"

I know "the house" is an old singlewide trailer with rooms added on each end. The entire structure has exterior wood paneling and a metal roof. It is a tinderbox.

Joe purchased it from our real estate company via a real estate contract, so I still have a financial interest in the house. More importantly, I have a personal interest in my partner.

"Are you OK?"

"Yes, I got out of the house with the clothes on my back. I moved my truck up the road but everything else is gone."

"What can I do for you?"

"Nothing at this point. I've called the fire company and they're on the way."

With that comment, his phone goes dead. I'm not surprised. The cell coverage in that area isn't very good.

I hang up the phone and sigh. Joe's wife had passed away 18 months earlier and now, he is losing every earthly possession he has except for his vehicle and the clothes on his back.

I open my office's window shade and, even though the house is three miles away, I see a pillar of smoke headed skyward. Helicopters from all three Albuquerque TV stations circle the smoke.

I reach for my TV remote, turn on the noon news, and watch the house burn.

Joe moves in with us for a few days before going to Texas to spend the holidays with his family.

Our family decides to see what we can salvage from the fire. Our intent is to clean those items and give them to Joe for a holiday present.

Joe lost many things in that fire. However, the only item we hear him bemoan losing is his late wife's wedding band.

We actually search the rubble several times. We find coins and military medals in a fireproof box. We do not find the ring.

We decide to search again on an unseasonably warm December afternoon.

We take several children, including Peter, with us.

Peter has seen angels for years. He has a connection to the spiritual realm that is unusual, even in our spiritual family.

We accept this at real, without doubt. We know that children often connect with the spiritual realm better than adults do and we hope Peter and his angels can help.

Children are more open to believing in something outside the normal realm of expectations because they haven't been educated to not believe. In addition, children are closer in the time dimension to the spiritual realm than adults are because they haven't lived as long in this life.

Peter usually sees angels out of the corner of his eye. They never say anything to him. They just show enough of their presence so that he knows they are there. He senses they are there to serve him.

We receive confirmation of his visions when we take a family vacation in 2002. During that trip, we visit a church in North Carolina that I helped start in the late 1980s. As we are preparing to leave, a stranger approaches the van. He apologizes for intruding but he says he has a message for us.

He tells us he senses something very special about our family. He talks about our role in society and the great things we will accomplish. He concludes by saying that our children will see angels and that "Mom and Dad should not doubt what the kids say about what they see."

We are confident Peter and his angels will discover the ring. We know it is in the rubble. We just don't know where. It is the ultimate search for the needle in the haystack.

Peter closes his eyes and asks the question, "Where is that ring?" He has used this technique before to find missing objects.

He asks the questions, stills his mind, and sees a picture of the missing item in its location. He then goes to the location and gets it.

Will his angels show him the ring?

Peter has confidence in his angels. They've never misled him. They serve as intermediaries to tell him God's direction. God could tell him directly. God could use an intermediary.

God can speak however how he/she wishes. In this case, God uses the angels.

Peter relaxes, closes his eyes, and sees a picture of the ring in its current location.

However, when he opens his eyes, he can't find the ring there.

The next day, we search again. We take a family friend with us and she finds the ring in the exact spot Peter saw. I explain why it took two people to accomplish this in the section, *Relationship Peace of Mind How to Live Within the Law of Attraction.*

For Joe's Christmas present that year, we purchase a little treasure chest and put all of the treasures we found in there - including that wedding band.

Giving it to him was a precious moment.

Conspiracy Question

Who or what are my Intermediaries?

Chapter 23

Peter knows he can trust his angels when they speak to him. Have you experienced similar events?

Do you trust your inner voice?

That inner voice speaks to you in multiple ways.

One of the ways it speaks to you is through your likes. It speaks to you through your Desires.

The likes and Desires you have today are one way the Divine speaks to you.

I believe you and God got together before you came to this life and discussed your Life Purpose.

You then worked together to program yourself with likes that would serve as clues for you to follow to achieve your Life Purpose.

Therefore...

You can trust your Desires – they are from God

The way to identify your major Desire – your Life Purpose – is to identify all of your likes

Then, to get a picture of what your main Desire (Life Purpose) is close your eyes and think of the answer to these questions:

What would I do if I could not fail?

What is the biggest thing I would do if I could?

If nothing comes to mind... just be patient – it will – maybe when you least expect it!

It may come later while reading this material. It may come tonight as you go to sleep. It may come the next time you step into the shower or drive you automobile.

And, when you receive the answer, you will discover that fulfilling that Desire means doing the things you like to do!

Let's review:

Your Major Desire allows you to experience everything you like.

Your likes lead you to your Major Desire (Life Purpose).

You can trust the supernatural forces that speak to you.

If you're not comfortable talking directly to God, it is OK to use intermediaries.

Of course, this raises the question of which intermediaries can you trust?

I'll answer that later in this book.

Now, let's look at what you can do to fulfill your Desire.

> **Conspiracy Question**
>
> What do I like?
>
> What do I like for my Relationships?
>
> What do I like for my Physical Build and Health?
>
> What do I like for my Money?
>
> What do I like for my Career? What do I like for my Recreation? What do I like for my Personal Skills?
>
> What do I like for my Contribution or Legacy?

Chapter 24

When I started writing this material, I thought I was experiencing The Law of Magic.

I now know that Miracles are not Magic.

There is a big difference between Magic and Miracles.

The dictionary describes "Magic" as the art that controls natural events by invoking the supernatural.

"Supernatural" is how we describe those things that happen outside of our five natural senses.

However, as science develops a greater ability to observe brainwaves, subatomic particles, and other previously unseen matter, science redefines supernatural. What once appeared supernatural is now natural because we understand that life functions at a molecular level.

This process is incremental and logical. The results appear to be Magic but they aren't. They are evidence of The Law of Attraction.

Just like a magician's trick, the results are easy to explain with a modest understanding of molecular science. In fact, I explain them in the section, *Relationship Peace of Mind How to Live Within the Law of Attraction.*

As I said, this process happens at the molecular level. It is incremental and logical.

The Law of Miracles uses the principles from the Law of Attraction. In addition, it operates at the quantum level.

The Law of Miracles is non-incremental and it feels illogical. It is not always predictable.

Later in this book, I go into detail about how The Law of Miracles works.

However, for now, let's look at how to use the Law of Attraction to move toward fulfilling your Desire.

Receiving your Desire is easy. It is natural… unless you create resistance.

For the twenty-three years prior to my experience in Baltimore, I learn to resist. My religion teaches me to resist things I enjoy because they might be "bad."

Even the things I know are "good" become difficult because of my resistance habit.

I habitually blame others for my struggles. I habitually live as a victim. I habitually create enemies. I habitually see barriers in everyone and everything.

Those habits stand between my Desire and me. I finally understand that to fulfill my Desire, I must change my habits.

To change habits, I must understand habits. I devote much of my free time to learning how to change my behavior.

I learn that at least eighty percent of my actions are habitual. The way I dress myself, how I get into bed at night, my speech patterns, and the way I brush my teeth are all behavioral habits.

If I carry on a conversation while driving my car, I participate in the habitual behavior of driving. I don't consciously think about the foot pressure I'm putting on the gas pedal or how much I have to turn the steering wheel to go around a corner. I do it by habit.

Those habits don't just happen. I program those habits through repetitive actions.

In addition, my life depends upon some habits. My heart and lungs function by habit. I have certain inborn instincts that qualify as behavior habits. These include blinking, smiling, scowling, and flinching. God programs those habits.

Once a habit forms, I do not have to be consciously aware to perform it. Therefore, by definition, the subconscious part of my brain controls those habits.

Scientific studies show that the subconscious makes up 5/6 of the brain. That part of my brain (83% of it) controls my habits, which are at least 80% of my actions.

That means my brain uses only 17% of its capacity for conscious behavior. The rest of my brain controls and manages my habitual behavior.

This is a problem if I consciously decide to change a habitual behavior. Eighty-three percent of my brain controls the habit and seventeen percent controls the decision to change the habit. The seventeen percent puts up a good fight but it always loses to the eighty-three percent because it is outmanned.

It seems hopeless. It feels as if fate has given me a certain place in life and I can do nothing about it. Carl Jung (Yung) addressed this very issue when he said

> *"Until you make the unconscious conscious, it will control your life and you will call it fate."*

However, I learn that if I have programmed old habits into my subconscious, I can program NEW habits into my subconscious to replace the old ones.

I do this through using thoughts, words, and actions to develop new habits. These thoughts, words, and actions become the tools I use to fulfill my Desire.

Conspiracy Question

What current habits do I have that keep me from fulfilling my Desire?

Chapter 25

I wish I could just work within the Law of Miracles, love all, and make this happen.

After all, that is the greatest truth.

However, once I learn the truth of The Law of Miracles, I don't experience it immediately.

It takes a while for my perception to change because I have habits.

The subconscious part of the brain – 83% of the brain controls these habits.

The good news is that since I programmed old habits into my subconscious, I can program NEW habits into my subconscious to replace the old ones.

I use my Desire to learn how to do that.

This plan works for my little likes and it works for my Life Purpose. It works for anything I Desire to accomplish.

Remember what I said about the brain.

It contains the conscious and subconscious.

The conscious part of my brain tries to make a change. However, the subconscious part usually interferes.

The subconscious interferes because it understands something that the conscious doesn't always understand.

The subconscious understands that thoughts and words are real things.

Great spiritual teachings tell us this. When I looked at those teachings as a list of dos and don'ts, I often rebelled against them.

However, once I understood that spiritual teachings explain how Universal laws work, I discover I am more likely to work with them.

Here are two examples of those teachings: "As a man thinks in his heart, so is he."

"Out of the abundance of the heart, the mouth speaks."

With this in mind, I learn thinking and speaking guidelines that integrate my thoughts, words, and actions.

I learn that my thoughts, words, and actions program my habits. I just need to change my thoughts, words, and actions to change my habits.

I start this change by creating a Success Environment. I believe it is possible for me to fulfill my Desire I give up the words "I can't."

I learn that what others think about me is none of my business because everyone is part of the Conspiracy to enhance my well-being.

I call this a "Conspiracy for Me."

I realize that every negative event contains the seed of an equal or greater benefit. It is all part of the Conspiracy

I look for the opportunity in everything. It is there because it is all part of the Conspiracy

If something happens differently than I hoped, I understand there must be something better for me because it is all part of the Conspiracy

For I while, I don't think I can succeed because I don't think I have succeeded previously. Therefore, I do a great little exercise to show me how I had previously succeeded.

I divided my life into three equal time periods. For me, I used birth to age 16, 17-31, and 32 to present.

Then, I wrote down three major successes for each time period.

Age 0-16

I passed all school grades without repeating any.

I made a baseball all-star team.
I made regional and all-county bands.

Age 17-31

I graduated from high school.
I graduated from college.
I married.

Age 32-present

I accomplished the life goal of eight kids.
I became debt free.
I built a dream home.

Then, I did another exercise to show me I could succeed. I created an award display area in my home.

I love sports. However, my parents were afraid I would be hurt if I played sports so they pushed me towards music. That way, I could watch sports free by performing music at the games.

I pursued music in college and my degree is in Music Education. However, in 1996, I had the opportunity to be assistant coach for a girls home school basketball team. That first-year team came within one basket of winning the New Mexico State Championship and won the Championship the next three years.

Then, I was offered the opportunity to be the head coach for the boys team.

This team previously experienced some success. However, it had never won a tournament or a championship. In the three years I coached, we won numerous tournaments, a New Mexico State Championship, and successfully competed against teams from all over the United States in regional and national tournaments.

In addition, the JV and C Team programs I started during those three years won several tournaments.

I have an attic of trophies from those years. Those trophies were in my office for a long time because they served as reminders of my successes.

They showed me that I could succeed.

Now, I have other reminders of success in my office including pictures of my family and a board that shows our daily income.

I know I can succeed today because I succeeded yesterday.
There are other tools available to programming my subconscious. I write about the most effective tool for me in the next chapter.

> **Conspiracy Question**
>
> When did I succeed?

Chapter 26

The best tool I have found for programming my subconscious is affirmations

Once I identify my likes, I turn them into affirmations.

An affirmation is a present tense statement of who I am, even though I may not yet be at that place in time. It includes specific actions and emotions. It includes the minimum standard of achievement and allows room for more.

For example:

> I am happily enjoying being a millionaire.

This affirmation carries an emotion (happiness) that allows me to visualize the results of being a millionaire.

I hear the sounds, smell the smells, and taste the tastes of being a millionaire.

I see myself living the lifestyle of a millionaire by the car I drive, the house I live in, the clothes I wear, the people I serve, and the money I give.

The brain sees no difference between visualizing something and actually doing it so I visualize as I say my affirmations.

I say my affirmations aloud once a day with my family.

You may say them aloud several times a day, once a day with your family, or immediately before you go to bed at night or after you get up in the morning.

However you decide to do it, the important thing to remember is that this is a tool to program your subconscious so that you live an integrated life.

This process moves you towards fulfilling your major Desire.

It worked for me in the past and it works for me in the present.

When I first learned about affirmations and experienced the benefits, I had to know why they worked so I did some research. Here is what I learned.

Anything that activates the creativity of my subconscious towards accomplishing my likes and Desires is a step in the right direction.

The reason is that I have an amazing system in my brain called the reticular activating system or RAS. (You have it too!)

I receive eight million bits of information at any one moment in time. This information from my five senses includes everything I see, hear, feel, taste, and smell. In addition, it includes everything going on within my body such as the respiratory, digestive, and circulatory systems.

The RAS filters out most of them and lets into my awareness only those signals that help me survive or accomplish my goals.

When I use affirmations, I program the RAS to notice available resources that were always there but previously unnoticed.

In addition, I magnetize myself with an energy that attracts the people, resources, and opportunities I need to achieve my goal.

There is even some evidence that when I focus on my goals, say affirmations, and visualize my success, I actually help my brain develop more of the brain cells that help with memory and success.

That takes care of thoughts and words. How do I use actions to program habits?

I act as if I have already reached that place in time in my affirmation.

For me, the emotions associated with being a millionaire come from the millionaire lifestyle.

Please understand that I don't kill myself financially while "acting as if."

I start by finding ways to act as if I'm there.

I quit purchasing cheap clothes. I wear the clothes I enjoy. I have fewer clothes so I still spend the same amount of money.

I love sports. My family enjoys movies. For us, the full cable TV package is a far better value than going to one ball game or one movie in a theatre.

I love great food so I go to nice restaurants and soak in the atmosphere. Then, I use a coupon to help pay for the meal.

The idea is to do things that feel luxurious and give me the feeling of being a millionaire.

As I do those things, I feel wealthy and my subconscious automatically does things that cause me to create wealth.

When I do those things regularly, they become habits.

If your affirmations are not tied to possessions or money, then imagine yourself in the perfect relationship or career or other situation that you Desire and use similar techniques.

If you need help with this process, use the resource information in the back of this book and request Peace of Mind Training Institute Coaching.

Let's review:

I must change my habits to fulfill my Desire.

I program my subconscious through using thoughts, words, and actions to change my habits.

I use affirmations and visualization to program my thoughts and words.

I think about all the details of my Desire. I close my eyes so I can easily feel the feelings, smell the smells, taste the tastes, and imagine all parts of my Desire.

I write statements describing situations where my Desire is reality. I write the feelings, describe the smells and tastes, and feel the emotions of having that Desire. I program my subconscious to think differently.

Those subconscious thoughts turn into words. I speak my written statements every day. I program myself to talk differently. Instead of creating resistance with my words, I relax. Instead of creating enemies, I speak words of love.

These words turn into new actions. Instead of building barriers, I remove them.

Those new actions turn into habits.

Behavior psychologists say it takes 21-30 days to develop a new habit. For me, some habits happen more quickly. Others take longer to develop.

One by one, I develop new habits. Each brings me closer to my Desire.

I don't know how this programming works. I just know that it works. My subconscious quits working against me.

I discover blocks to this process. They are blocks I created. I write about those blocks next.

> **Conspiracy Activity**
>
> Review the habit you identified in Chapter 24. Write an affirmation to overcome that habit.

Chapter 27

I am not surprised at the reality of my mom's potential death but I am surprised at the message I receive on that summer day in August 2007.

I believe that we choose when we will die. I know the soul does not make that decision lightly. It isn't that the soul fears death. It doesn't. However, the soul knows that those left behind may not understand.

My surprise comes in the specificity of the message. "Will she really die before the wedding?" I ask.

"That's up to her. She feels badly that she won't be there for the wedding and she needs a legitimate excuse for not attending. Death is a good excuse."

I think about that statement.

I learned as a child to use sickness to get out of doing almost anything. I suppose I learned that skill from my Mother. She always worked when sick so I can't say that she did that herself. However, she usually allowed me to get away with that technique so she was sympathetic to it.

It makes sense that she would do that in this situation.

The voice continues. "You are not to ruin the day for your daughter. In fact, you must not tell anyone if it happens. Enjoy the day and make any travel arrangement after the wedding. Do not even tell your wife."

I envision myself following those instructions. They are consistent with my current efforts to remove all drama from my life. They make sense.

Mary, my daughter, became pregnant in May and the emotions from her pregnancy combined with the emotions of her wedding day do not need complication from the knowledge of her Grandmother's death.

I feel no sadness over the message and instructions. I believe that we live forever. I know that is true for my mom too.

Two days later, on Tuesday afternoon, Sheri and I have a

conversation. The topic is how we recreate ourselves every day. We discuss her father's health and my mother's health. I tell her about my conversation with "the voice." I finish by saying that I won't tell her about Mom's health until after the wedding.

I wonder if I have said too much to her but I sense that I need someone to know what I knew so I wouldn't appear to just be "making it up" after it happened.

As the weekend and the wedding day draw closer, I wonder if maybe I had just made it up. I attempt to put all of those thoughts to rest, knowing I can do nothing about someone else's death.

However, the subject won't go away.

Several friends ask me numerous questions about death throughout the week. The subject is on my mind and I am attracting the conversations. What is going to happen?

On Friday morning, my youngest daughter, Esther, comes into my office. It is her birthday and our family tradition is that the children call Grandma and Grandpa and receive birthday wishes.

I dial the number for my daughter on the desk phone and hand the cordless phone to Esther. In a couple of minutes, she says, "They didn't answer the phone."

I think to myself, "It is Friday morning. Mom might be grocery shopping."

An hour later, we try again with the same results.

An hour later, my cell phone rings. I don't recognize the number. However, I recognize the area code. It is the one for my Mom's hometown.

> **Conspiracy Question**
>
> What health problems do I experience when I face outside difficulties or conflicts?

Chapter 28

"Matthew, its Mom. I'm in Roanoke Memorial Hospital. I had a heart attack."

As the story unfolds, I realize that just 36 hours earlier Mom wrestled with death.

Truthfully, she didn't wrestle with death. She wrestled with her Desire.

After a couple hours, she decided to live.

The medical staff wasn't sure she would live at first. They tell her afterwards they were all scared for her.

However, when the results of the heart catheterization and subsequent tests arrive, the cardiologist is amazed. He says her arteries are the clearest he has ever seen in one of his patients. There is no obvious medical reason for what caused her heart attack.

Thanks to the information I received during my meditation, I know the answers that no amount of medical testing can reveal.

She didn't have to die to not attend the wedding. A heart attack was enough of an excuse.

That brings me Peace of Mind. Why?

Sickness and death are two of the things we fear the most in our society. I believe her story demonstrates that a person determines the timing of his or her death.

In addition, it demonstrates that a person determines the timing and intensity of his or her sickness.

My mother is a deeply religious woman. Unfortunately, that religious perspective teaches her right and wrong, good and evil. It forces her to dance around the blocks in her thinking.

She Desired to be at her granddaughter's wedding. She felt guilty for not being there.

She blamed the distance for not being able to attend.

She was afraid of flying and other means of travel are no longer viable to her.

Those conflicting thoughts combined to give her the symptoms of a heart attack.

I say symptoms because there is no medical reason why she had a heart attack.

She experienced the greatest obstacles to The Law of Miracles. Those obstacles are the emotions of guilt, blame, and fear.

My mom's religion is the one I learned as a kid. It programmed me early in my life.

My observation is that most people in our society have the same programming.

Here is my experience. I suspect yours is similar. My religion teaches love and fear.

It follows the marketing formula of create a problem, agitate the problem, and sell the solution.

Unfortunately, the solution my religion offers is only temporary because a permanent solution would put religion out of business.

Therefore, religion teaches both love and fear by focusing on duality. It teaches guilt and forgiveness, bondage and freedom.

The bondage and guilt comes from sin.

My religion teaches that everyone sins and everyone must feel guilty about it before experiencing forgiveness. This emotional pendulum swinging is the primary cause of blocks to changing my habits.

I learned this belief system from my religion and it held me back for the first forty years of my life.

The reason is simple. My belief system determines my success. It determines my Peace of Mind.

Every time I have coached someone and met resistance, it was because of his or her belief system.

Every time I experienced resistance in my attempt to move forward, it was because of my belief system.

I kept tracing it back to a single source. It is this religious teaching. Every conflict comes from the religious teaching of a God of love who rules by fear

This produces the teaching that I'm a slave to sin and I should feel guilty about it so I can experience forgiveness.

In addition, I need to forgive other people when they sin against me.

Religion teaches forgiveness as the emotional release

I discover that is hard to do. I apologize – that's a lie. It isn't hard to do. It is IMPOSSIBLE to do.

However, religion keeps teaching it and holding it up as an unobtainable goal because it is a good marketing strategy.

It creates a need that is impossible to meet.

I learn to experience guilt. I never experience complete forgiveness so I blame others.

When I blame other people or other situations, I give away my personal power including the responsibility for the results in my life.

This guilt and blame keeps me living in the past.

I become afraid of repeating what caused the guilt. I am also afraid of the punishment of past sins and future sins. I know I'll be punished by sickness and death. My religion teaches that to me.

Yes, my religion offers me eternal life but it is almost impossible to obtain. I'll be punished with death if I sin and since sickness sometimes leads to death, I see sickness as that punishment too.

That fear is a self-fulfilling prophecy for my actions.

I make more mistakes, feel more guilt, blame more people, experience more fear, and repeat.

I only see glimpses of freedom, love, and forgiveness.

After more than thirty-five years of this double-minded life, I learn a secret. This secret challenges much of what I think is true so it takes me a while to believe it and even longer to act on it.

However, when I believe it and start acting on it, I finally experience Peace of Mind. In addition, I experience love and the resulting Miracles!

> **Conspiracy Questions**
>
> What do I feel guilty about today?
>
> Whom do I blame for my failures, pains, and discomfort?
>
> What fears do I have?

Chapter 29

The secret I learn is that I always do my best. There are no mistakes.

My best may change as I process stimuli in my environment. I learn more, I experience more, and my best changes.

My best is different when I am tired as opposed to when rested. However, I always do my best in the present moment.

If this is true for me, this is true for other people also. They always do their best. Deep down, no one wants to make mistakes. No one wants to hurt other people. Everyone wants what is best for them and those around them.

In the past, my sin consciousness and the fear of a mistake limited my power.

However, when I learn that I have never made a mistake, things change.

I learn that when I thought I had made a mistake, I hadn't.

The reason is that after the incident, I gleaned knowledge from it. While the incident was still in progress, I operated on the basis of the best information that I had at the time.

In truth, I couldn't have known any better and, therefore, there is no reason to beat myself up over it.

I learned a lesson. However, I did not make a mistake.

Learning a lesson and making a mistake are two entirely different things. Lessons don't carry the same feelings as mistakes. There's no guilt attached to our lessons. Mistakes imply that we've done something wrong.

Once I learn that I've never done anything wrong, everything changes.

I learn there is no value in placing moral judgments on events in my life.

The concept of right and wrong is simply an illusion that doesn't exist for me unless I nourish it. I can choose to plead not guilty to all of the menacing "should haves" that charge me with wrongdoing.

In my mind, I can assert that everything is all right regardless of what others may say, and, in doing so, I return to the innocence I had at birth.

I learn I am responsible for my happiness. I don't feel guilt or obligation in regard to other people. It isn't my fault if I inadvertently "make them unhappy." They are only relating to me according to their experiences and their processes.

Limited knowledge or limited perspective may encourage me to do something that could be interpreted as a mistake or that could be called harmful.

However, the truth is, we always do our best. I always do my best. You always do your best. Everybody always does his or her best.

As I learn this, I mean really learn it, I become free from guilt, blame, and fear.

If I always do my best and I don't make mistakes, there is no need for guilt.

The reason is no mistakes means no sin. No sin means no guilt.

In addition, if I am not guilty, there is no need to blame others. They always do their best and they don't make mistakes either.

This way of thinking completely changes the way I look at forgiveness. When I know everyone does his or her best, I do not experience guilt so I can easily "forgive" myself.

In addition, since I no longer have a need to blame others, I can easily "forgive" others.

When the guilt and blame disappear, fear disappears too because there is no fear of punishment. In addition, the fear of sickness and death go away because they are no longer punishment for sin. They are simply doorways to the next experience.

> **Conspiracy Question**
>
> When was the last time I morally judged my actions or someone else's?

(I share more insights on sickness and death in the section, *Financial Peace of Mind – How to Live Within The Law of Abundance.*)

Learning that I do my best has many benefits. I saved the best benefit for last…

Chapter 30

I discover another benefit to my new way of thinking. I learn how to love.

I demonstrate love whenever I am present in the moment. I pay attention to those around me without distractions.

I cannot be present if I am feeling guilty about the past or blaming someone about the past or worrying about the future.

By staying in the moment, I recognize I can only do one thing at a time well. It means I stay focused on that one thing while doing it.

Some spiritual writings describe this as living in the eternal where time doesn't exist.

This is a little tricky to understand because I live in the dimension of time. I see things sequentially.

However, when I realize the current experience is part of the overall experience that is still in progress, I forget about the results and I can focus on the moment, not worry about the future, and lay aside the past.

This allows me to realize mistakes do not exist because this is still a work on progress.

The blame goes away. The guilt goes away. I easily forgive because there is no harm.

Frankly, I believe this is the message of Jesus. It is the message of Mohammad. It is the message of Buddha. It is the message of Moses and Solomon. It is the message of all spiritual teachings.

Religion serves as an intermediary to bring us closer to that message. For some of us, that is enough.

It isn't enough for me.

I Desire to experience the Miracle of love that comes through a direct connection to my Inner Source. Love allows Miracles to take place.

Love allows shortcuts through time and space.

You read in earlier chapters about how I learned to use my thoughts, words, actions, and habits to receive my Desire.

I move slowly through time and space, creeping ever so slowly toward my Desire. I learn principals of manifesting. I intend. I affirm. I practice.

As I go through this process, I experience life. I learn lessons. I grow. I love.

Then, suddenly, without warning, a Miracle takes place. I accomplish more in a day than I accomplished in the previous year.

Quantum physicists call it a quantum leap. I am at one place and suddenly, I am at another place. Normally, it would take hours or days to make that move. However, the move is instantaneous, without time advancing, and without any memory of going through space.

Love causes the leap. It is The Law of Miracles.

Sometimes, mentors assist those leaps. These mentors are special beings who show up at just the right time.

When the student is ready, the teacher will appear.

I am one of your mentors. The reason I know this is that you are reading this material today. The Law of Attraction brought you and me together.

I have numerous mentors. Every person in your life is a mentor. In addition, every being in your life is a mentor.

Conspiracy Question

What Miracle have I experienced in my life?

Chapter 31

Beings such as the ones that helped Peter find the ring and the ones that spoke to me during the week before my daughter's wedding are supernatural mentors

I call them "virtual mentors."

Some people are uncomfortable with the supernatural realm, so the "virtual mentor" title makes this concept easier to accept. Most people believe virtual mentors exist.

Those people who don't believe they exist usually float in the water of an Egyptian River – They are in denial (The Nile).

I do not know anyone who has not experienced something that defies natural explanation.

For example, have you ever experienced a dream, levitation, an unusual healing, supernatural financial supply, or someone calling just as you think of them?

I'm sure you have because everyone has. It is actually a normal occurrence.

Therefore, the question really isn't "Do supernatural things happen?"

The question is, "Why do supernatural things happen and can I trust them?"

The reason I bring up this question is that people usually think of two types of supernatural beings: angels and demons. Angels can be trusted. Demons cannot be trusted.

Before I answer this, I must tell you that I've participated in exorcisms. I've seen things that appeared to be horribly evil and demonic. I write about those things in the section, Personal Peace of Mind, How to Live Within The Law of Attraction.

Therefore, I don't share this information with you lightly. It has much experience behind it. I've thought over it and through it for many years. I am 100% certain of this answer.

If I always do my best, if you always do your best, if everyone always does his or her best, does it make sense that virtual mentors always do their best too.

Think about it...

How would a virtual mentor benefit by harming you? Can you think of a way? I can't think of one either.

Receiving guidance from Virtual Mentors (the supernatural realm) can be controversial because it is a spiritual experience. We traditionally write rules about our spiritual experiences and call them religions.

(For more information about virtual mentors, read the next chapter.)

The problem with this practice is that we label anything outside of those rules as "wrong" or "evil."

We have already established that everyone always does his or her best. We've already established that there are no mistakes, no sin, and no guilt.

Therefore, there is no wrong way or evil way to hear from virtual mentors.

In the two years prior to writing this material, I received guidance from mediums, tarot readers, books, God, Pleiades, songs, mentors, movies, games, birds, dogs, orbs, and many other sources.

My reticular activating system brings me the exact information I need at just the time I need it.

From September through December of 2008, I experience the following events.

> *A friend I haven't seen in 25 years comes across the country and visits me. As my friend leaves, she hands me a book. The book has a quote in it that answers a question I have struggled with for more than ten years.*
>
> *A client introduces me to a friend who needs accounting help. This friend is a medium who, during*

our first phone call, tells me about my body's condition over the phone. This person has never met me. However, they know my body as well as me.

I meet someone online, we meet for coffee, and this person tells me how to treat the physical condition diagnosed by the first person.

Two other friends hand me books to read. These books give me increased insight into the material I am writing.

I take a writing course and a friend who doesn't know I'm taking the course questions my commitment to something in my life. They don't know what it is. They just have a sense about it. When I look closely, I realize I'm not fully participating in the writing course.

These series of events are just one example of the Conspiracy for Me. They combine virtual mentors with human beings to provide shortcuts through time and space – a Miracle

Each Miracle brings me closer to my fulfilled Desire.

I believe it all. I do it all. It is a giant Conspiracy for me. It brings me Peace of Mind.

Personal Peace of Mind comes when I understand that all Desires come from God – they may be trusted.

Personal Peace of Mind comes when I move towards fulfilling those Desires by integrating myself through using The Law of Attraction.

Personal Peace of Mind comes when I realize that everyone does his or her best. I love all. I trust all. I experience Miracles that produce quantum leaps.

Personal Peace of Mind comes when I participate in the Conspiracy for Me to fulfill my Desire.

> **Conspiracy Questions**
>
> What supernatural events have I experienced?
>
> How have I received guidance from virtual mentors?

Chapter 32

Questions and Answers about Virtual Mentors

My intent with this article is to provide answers to common questions based on my experience. These are not hard and fast rules. I understand that your experiences may be different. However, I hope these answers are helpful for you as you seek to receive guidance from your Virtual Mentors.

How do you hear from the supernatural?

It would be easier to list how I do NOT hear from the supernatural. I believe everything that happens in my life is a message for me. The key for me is awareness. If I am aware of what takes place around me, I always hear the message.

Does that mean the messages always come from outside you?

No, messages come from inside me also. In fact, I believe that my innermost being knows exactly what I need and connects with the rest of the Universe to bring that into my life. Some of those messages come though other people, beings and events. Some of those messages come from inside me.

How do you hear those inside messages?

I usually set aside 30-60 minutes every day to meditate. I do this while sitting in the hot tub or sun bathing. In the past, I have done this while driving or taking a shower. I quit thinking, still my mind, and listen.

What do you hear?

Sometimes, it is a dialogue in my head between two voices. At other times, a new idea or a reminder of an old idea just pops into my head. If I am in a place where I can close my eyes, I may see visions.

What do those visions look like?

Sometimes, I just see a glimmer of something. At others times, it appears as a vivid dream where I am a participant. On other occasions, I see something like a movie screen appear and I just watch without participating.

Do you have to meditate to hear or see the messages?

No, I can see or hear them at any time. I often receive them while having a conversation, writing, and speaking publicly. I see meditation as practice so that I can easily recognize those messages during "real life' events.

Do you receive the messages other than through voices or visions?

Yes, I receive messages through my Desires. I believe all Desires are divinely inspired. I recognize my Desires through positive, high frequency emotions such as joy, peace, etc. Negative emotions such as anger, fear, etc. are not my Desires.

How do you guard against evil messages?

I don't believe that evil messages exist so I don't receive them.

Do some of the messages make you afraid?

No, the messages always bring peace. Fear, anger, etc. are the result of how I think other people may respond when I follow my Desires or act on my messages.

Do you receive conflicting messages?

No, the messages are always clear and confirming. If I perceive a conflict, I know that I need more information so I take time to meditate and find an answer.

Do you ever receive wrong guidance?

Wrong is an opinion, based on perspective. My experience is that whenever I thought I received "wrong" guidance, it became correct as I matured and my perspective changed. Therefore, I can honestly say I have never received "wrong guidance."

What can I do to receive messages more often?

Act on what you hear. I find that if I'm not acting, there is nothing further for my mentor to tell me.

Do you ever feel like you are making up your messages?

Yes, I always feel that way because, since I am part of the Universe, I am. My reticular activation system makes me aware of the messages. The messages come to answer the questions that are on my mind. The exciting news is that since I am connected to the Universe, the messages are not limited to my personal experience and knowledge. All I have to do is tap into that vast wealth of knowledge to receive answers to questions.

If you want to know more about this subject, I am available for private consultations and group sessions. Please use the material in the back of the book for more information.

Chapter 33

Listening to My Desire and Intuition

In the previous chapters, you discovered you can trust your Desire and your intuition.

For years, I only wish I can trust my intuition completely. The problem is that my intuition was wrong one time when I was 6 years old so, I don't trust it.

Since that experience in 1968, I overanalyze every feeling, every emotion to see if it is right or wrong. Please let me explain.

As a little boy, I develop a crush on a cute little girl in my class. I'll call her Cathy.

We go through school together from second grade through graduation and the crush remains. I never act on it because, in my mind, Cathy is out of my league.

I don't know her very well so there is no logical reason for the crush. We seldom talk and when we do, it is about class assignments. It is purely business. Our social paths never cross. I'm in band and choir. Cathy is a cheerleader.

The crush never leaves. My inability to act on my crush teaches me my intuition can be wrong.

Every so often, my parents ask me if I ever hear from Cathy. They know about my crush and they sense it is still there. Even though I'm married and have a family, my parents still ask.

Their questions remind me that my intuition cannot be trusted.

I write Living the Southwest Lifestyle material. I teach that Desires can always be trusted because they are from God (Desire means "of the Father"). I explain that integrity is spirituality without exception.

Still, there is a lingering doubt in the back of my mind. I have a crush on Cathy and we don't even know each other.

I try to write it off as a mistake, something to correct. However, it won't leave.

Then, in November 2008, I join several social internet sites. My intent is to establish networks to market my writings.

The friend requests arrive from acquaintances, classmate, and clients. I recognize all but one. I research this person and discover we were in school together. Could it be her?

We trade greetings. It is Cathy.

The old feelings return. What is going on here?

I'm so excited I tell my friends and family about it. I tell my parents I've heard from Cathy. They don't say much. They seem to know this would happen.

We trade a few more messages. Once again, the communication is "purely business."

It is like old times. The communication reminds me that my intuition can be wrong.

I try not to think about it. I try to put it behind me. I'm successful doing this on the conscious level.

However, I discover the doubts still linger on the subconscious level.

Finally, I decide to give my intuition another chance. I write and send the following email.

> *Being in touch with you again brings back many memories. I hope you don't mind if I share some of them with you.*
>
> *My memories start in the 2nd grade class we share. At some point during that year, I develop a crush on you.*
>
> *Whenever someone mentions your name or I see you, the butterflies rush into my tummy and I am*

entranced.

You become the "rich girl in the mansion that I have the crush on" and I watch from a distance.

The distance isn't about how you treat me. You are always kind to me. The distance is about my insecurities and my perspective of being a poor kid who isn't in your league.

We go to different schools for the next three years. Then, in sixth grade, we are back in school together. Again, whenever someone mentions your name or I see you, the butterflies rush into my tummy and I am entranced.

My perspective doesn't change. I stay on the fringe of your life, afraid to enter into it.

As we go through school, our paths cross many times. The butterflies always return. I always stay on the fringe.

Time goes by, we go our separate ways, move away from our hometown, marry, and live our lives.

Then, a few weeks ago, almost thirty years after my last contact with you, you send a friend request to me. Once I figure out the identity of Cathy Barnes, the butterflies return en masse. I am stunned.

During the past thirty years, my perspective has changed a great deal. I don't hide behind fears or insecurities. I know that my emotions are the voice of my soul and I'm learning to listen, really listen, to them. I decide to accept the friend request. I tell you that you made my day.

Truthfully, you made my MONTH!

Then, with every little message, the butterflies flutter. This is a busy time of the year for me so I don't respond to them. I focus on my work.

However, when you post pictures recently, the butterflies turn into something larger, something grander, something I still can't describe, and something I can no longer ignore.

Looking back, my crush on you wasn't a physical or sexual attraction. It was a "soul cry" of some type, something I can't really explain. It wasn't logical or reasonable. However, it was real to me.

Now, I realize it never left. It still isn't logical or reasonable. However, it is real to me so I have to respond.

The pictures show your spirit, your heart, your... I don't know how to put it into words but I see something in those pictures that is very special.

I keep those pictures open in my browser all morning Friday and stare at them often; trying to figure out what it is about them, about you that entrances me.
I don't know the answer...yet.

As I think about it over the weekend, I know that I have to tell you. If I have any doubts, they disappear when, without prompting, my wife says, "You need to tell her. She needs to know."

So, I have.

If we lived closer to one another, I'd suggest we meet for coffee or lunch so we could talk. We would catch up on the past and compare each other's journey. I suspect it wouldn't take long to figure out why I have this "soul cry" for you.

However, because of the distance, the best I can do at this point is to send you an email, describe my experiences, and see if you are open to starting a dialogue. I believe there is a significant reason that I have these feelings and it goes beyond a childhood crush.

> *Perhaps you have something to teach me, I have something to teach you, or maybe it is something that will completely surprise both of us.*
>
> *I look forward to hearing from you. With great admiration,*
>
> *Matthew*

When I send the email, I sense a shift inside me. I walk away from the computer and release any attachment to the results. Maybe my intuition is trustworthy. After all, my wife's intuition confirms my intuition. Maybe I can trust it.

I discover I am at peace.

Less than two hours later, I have a response. I open it without hesitation.

Cathy, the object of my crush, is at a loss for words. She had no idea of my feelings. She insists on calling me the next week.

I respond and she calls the next day.

In fact, we talk several times that week.

We catch up on our past.

We share spiritual stores.

We laugh.

We cry.

A weight comes off my shoulders as I realize that my intuition wasn't wrong. In fact, it was completely accurate.

Cathy and I have a great deal to offer one another. She teaches a discipline that I just started learning. My writing confirms her discoveries.

During our conversations, Cathy mentions several books. One resonates with me. I know I have to get it.

I use the internet to put it on hold at the library before we finish our conversation.

I pick it up the next day and read it in one night.

I find everything else written by the author and put all of his books on hold.

I pick them up and read them. My wife reads them. Our children read them.

Every book is jammed full of insight on following intuition. Suddenly, I trust everything coming from my intuition without a trace of doubt. I act without hesitation. Everything in my life accelerates.

It is easier to hear my intuition because I trust it. I no longer block it.

My relationships experience fulfillment because trusting my intuition is necessary before I can trust others.

My businesses experience remarkable profit during "down economic times" because I take massive action immediately instead of overanalyzing what my intuition tells me.

I suddenly have the courage to close a profitable business because it distracts me from my passion of writing and coaching.
I schedule two weeks of training to help my sons with their business.

Life becomes easy, so easy that I wonder each day what remarkable thing will come my way today.

Even though I wasn't conscious of it, my unfulfilled childhood crush subconsciously hindered me from trusting my internal guidance. It prevented me from clearly hearing my source, my God. This happens because I think it was wrong once.

Truthfully, I just didn't have all the facts yet.

Today, I know it wasn't wrong then and it won't be wrong tomorrow. Learning to trust my intuition moves my life to a new level.

I wonder what remarkable thing will come my way today.

Oh – and as a follow up to that story, several months later, Cathy and her husband, who live 1500 miles away from us just happened to take a vacation close enough to New Mexico so that my wife and I could spend a day with them.

We had a wonderful time together and I suspect we haven't seen the last of them.

Relationship Peace of Mind

*How to Live Within
The Law of Attraction*

Chapter 34

"Matt, the devil is talking through him."

I look up to see Pam, a small brunette, bust through the door with a visitor. She had left our prayer circle just a few minutes earlier to find the person who had arrived at the door and left.

She and I had seen the outline of the figure in the crack between the double doors. She was compelled to go see who it was.

In the fall of 1983, a small of group of college students and young adults agreed to meet each evening at 10:30 PM to pray for the campus and community. Our vision was to take the campus for Christ and to battle against the principalities and powers of darkness.

In other words, wage war against the demonic.

We met throughout the fall semester of that school year and continued meeting during the spring semester. Midway through the spring, we heard rumors of demonic activity and exorcisms.

However, we had never seen any visual evidence of the demonic realm. We didn't realize that was about to change.

When Pam left the prayer circle that evening, she went out the double doors of the small auditorium and through the glass doors of the East Carolina University Art Building. From the landing, at the top of the exterior stairs, she saw a lone figure walking east on the sidewalk.

She went down the stairs to catch up with the young man. It was Kevin, a stocky, former high school wrestler.

Kevin sometimes attended the nightly prayer meetings. However, he had not attended lately.

He looked awful. If Pam hadn't known him, she would have been afraid.

Instead, Pam attempted to hug him. Kevin reached out to her and as soon as they made contact, a low growl escaped his throat.
He hissed as he pushed her away and said, "Get away from me. I

hate you... you Christians."

Pam responded by saying, "I bind you in Jesus' Name." She then put Kevin into a headlock, dragged him back to the art building, up the stairs, through the glass doors, and into the back of the auditorium where we were still praying.

The pair was quite a sight. Pam, her green eyes wide with excitement, and Kevin, who was both taller and heavier, bent over under the force of Pam's right arm, his blonde hair standing on end.

The prayer circle moved towards them and the exorcism began. That was the first of many demonic experiences for our small group. During the next six months, we saw and experienced things that most people think only happen in the movies.

I'll tell you more about these experiences later in this book. For now, I promise that, no matter how difficult your relationship experiences are, that even if you suspect other parties in your relationship might be demon possessed, this material will bring you Peace of Mind in your relationships.

Conspiracy Question

What do I feel the need to fight against?

Chapter 35

By the time you finish reading this book, you will understand how The Law of Attraction works in relationships.

In addition, you will be able to use this material to build healthy, positive, and peaceful relationships.

Before I go further, I need to explain that if you don't have 100% peaceful relationships now, this material may seem radical. This book contains deeply personal stories that may challenge your life- long convictions. They may rub you the wrong way. They may make you dreadfully uncomfortable.

Just remember this. The results in your life came from what you did in the past. If you don't like what you have now, you must do something differently to get different results.

Take a deep breath and let's dive in.

The Law of Attraction states that Attraction happens automatically through the principle of sympathetic vibration.

Later in this book, you will learn how to use this law. First, let's learn how this law works.

Science demonstrates that all items constantly vibrate. Items that appear to be solid consist of vibrating molecules. Thoughts and words vibrate. There are no proven exceptions.

These vibrations take place as waves. Waves vibrating at the same frequency are said to be "in sympathy" with one another. The term for this is "sympathetic vibration."

The root word for "sympathetic" is "sympathy." When you feel sympathy towards someone, you feel what he or she feels because the two of you vibrate at the same frequency.

This shared energy appears magical because it produces amazing results. These results include healthy relationships, beautiful music, and architectural wonders.

If you have previously read my material or heard me speak, you have heard the story of how my wife, Sheri, and I started our relationship.

I was working as director of a Christian coffeehouse. My responsibilities included playing keyboards in a music group and writing original music for songs. Sometimes I wrote the words and other times, the words came from other people.

In the fall of 1984, I have a beautiful musical accompaniment but no words. No one else has words either. Nothing fits the music. As fall turns into winter, a new female attendee at the coffeehouse approaches and says, "You write music don't you?"

I say "yes."

"See what you can do with this" is her reply and she hands me a sheet of lined paper with handwritten words.

I thank her and tuck away the paper. The next time I play the piano; I pull out the paper and try the new words with my new music. Amazingly, the words fit perfectly with the music. I don't have to change a syllable or a note.

The writer of these words for my music is Sheri.

We spend time together over the next few weeks polishing the song so she can sing it for a Sunday morning church service.

Our relationship grows out of this time together and within three months, we recognize we share similar Desires. We decide to spend the rest of our life together accomplishing those Desires. That is the Law of Attraction at work.

It is logical. It is easy to explain. It is The Law of Attraction. The Law of Attraction has three elements. They are:

1. My Emotional Intensity Is More Important Than The Emotion
2. My Perspective Determines What I See
3. I Always Get What I Desire

Conspiracy Question

What causes me to feel emotional?

Chapter 36

ELEMENT ONE: Emotional Intensity Is More Important Than The Emotion

The Law of Attraction uses emotional energy. Feelings of love, hate, passion, or anger towards something give power to that item and attract it to you.

Notice that the key is not the type of emotion. The key is the intensity of the emotion.

Love and hate both attract because both are strong emotions producing strong energy.

Any emotion - love, hate, anger, passion, fear, joy - contains energy. The more intense the feeling, the more energy it contains.

The word emotion has motion in it.

Likewise, when you feel emotion, you move.

All movement consists of wave energy or vibrations. The more emotion you feel, the more you move, the more waves you create. This is simple physical science applied to life.

Let's look at how this works in a personal relationship.

Before I go further, you need to understand something. You cannot manipulate other people through the Law of Attraction. You can attract certain circumstances into your life such as a committed relationship with a loving person. However, if the person you are currently with is not interested in a committed relationship with a loving person, they will be repelled from you.

The Law of Attraction does not change other people. It attracts those who Desire what you Desire and repels those who don't Desire what you Desire.

Have you ever experienced a relationship going sour? The natural reaction is to grumble and complain about it. You might even go talk to your friends about it. You focus on how bad it is.

What happens? It gets even worse. The fights intensify. The arguments increase. You grumble and complain about it to your friends. You continue focusing on how bad it is and it gets even worse!

Your emotional energy towards the negative part of the relationship actually increases the likelihood that the relationship will get worse. All your complaining and grumbling give it extra energy.

The personal relationship becomes worse as you dwell on the unpleasant parts because you empower it to do that. The result is one of two things. Either the other person stays because he wants an unpleasant relationship or the other person leaves because he does not want an unpleasant relationship.

Did you see that? Your emotional focus on the unpleasant part of the relationship either increases the intensity of the unpleasantness or drives the other person away. In fact, the only way he will stay is to fight with you. Otherwise, he is gone!

On the other hand, a pleasant personal relationship becomes better as you dwell on the pleasant parts of it. The emotions you feel empower the relationship to remain positive. If the other person wants a pleasant relationship, he stays. However, if he does not want to participate in a pleasant relationship, he leaves.

You attract more of what you think about because of the vibrations in your thoughts.

Prior to the time I meet Sheri, I emit energy through thoughts and words. I write music that attracts her lyrics. She writes lyrics that attract my music. The energy created by the vibration of the piano strings radiate to her words so that by the time she gives them to me, they fit perfectly.

The Law of Attraction is strong. Sympathetic vibration is powerful.

> **Conspiracy Question**
>
> What three emotions do I feel the most?

Chapter 37

Another term for sympathetic vibration is resonance.

I first notice the power of resonance in the early 1970s when Memorex asks the question "Is it live, or is it Memorex?" In the famous television commercials, Ella Fitzgerald sings a note that shatters a glass. Memorex records the singing onto a Memorex audio cassette. The playing back of the tape also breaks the glass.

As a kid, I thought loud volume broke the glass. I now know that it was not volume. Instead, Ella sung a note that vibrated at the same wavelength as the glass. This caused the glass to vibrate. The energy of the vibrating glass increased as Ella continued to sing until the structure of the glass shattered.

A few years later, a film shown during a high school physics class about the Tacoma Narrows Bridge gives me the next lesson on sympathetic vibration.

Architects and engineers did not fully understand sympathetic vibration when they built the Tacoma Narrows Bridge in 1940. They knew that a bridge in Manchester England collapsed in 1831 when soldiers marched on it. The marching vibrated in resonance with the bridge and caused a wave so large that the bridge collapsed.

However, architects and engineers did not consider the effects of sympathetic vibration caused by unseen forces on a suspension bridge. As a result, sympathetic vibration caused by wind collapsed the Tacoma Narrows Suspension Bridge months after it opened.

My sympathetic vibration lessons continue during college as I earn a degree in Music Education. There, I discover that stringed instruments demonstrate sympathetic vibration.

I demonstrate this in my live presentations using a tuned guitar. I pluck the high E string - the smallest string on the guitar. Then, I put my finger against it to kill the vibration and the sound.

However, the sound continues because several other strings on the guitar vibrate from the energy produced by the high E string. The low E string plus the A and B strings produce sound even though I did not pluck them.

These examples clearly demonstrate sympathetic vibration. This phenomenon works in all parts of life. The reason is that everything contains wave energy.

The way I remember this is through the expression, "What I focus on expands." This is true even if I focus on things I do NOT like. Those things become larger and more powerful in my life because I give them extra attention.

I create energy when I focus on the things I love. I create energy when I focus on the things I hate. Either way, I create energy that sends out a wave and attracts those things to me.

Once I understand this, my next question is, "How should I respond when faced with something I dislike?" I discuss this in the next chapter.

> **Conspiracy Question**
>
> What three emotions do I feel most intensely?
>
> This material is explained in greater detail at the **Peace of Mind Training Institute Seminars**. To learn more, visit www.peaceofmindtraininginstitute.com

Chapter 38

If the Law of Attraction is true, I attract everything into my life, even the things I dislike.

How does this happen?

The easiest way to answer this question is through a series of events that took place in January 2009.

I receive my monthly "With Forgiveness" email during the first week of the New Year.

Sheri Rosenthal and Susyn Reeve combine each month to write messages of forgiveness and encouragement.

(If you want to know more about their work, go to www.WithForgiveness.com.)

I first encountered their work several years ago through a daily series of emails. The messages inspired me enough to forward the link to my family and suggest that each person also sign up to receive the series.

I'm glad I did. My oldest son, Emmanuel, learned a valuable lesson because of those messages.

A few months later, my wife, Sheri, and I had a wonderful dinner in Sedona, Arizona with Susyn. She has a residence in the area. She was in between visits to faraway places and "just happened" to be there on the night we were passing through.

I believe it was a divine appointment.

The conversation that evening brought a new freedom to my writing and generated a book idea for my wife.

In addition, I learned about Don Miguel Ruiz and *The Four Agreements.*

Looking back, I see those few hours as life changing. I still receive unexpected benefits from that visit with Susyn.

I respect Susyn and Sheri.

Therefore, whenever they make a recommendation, I must consider it.

January's email had a reference to the website www.ITakeTheVow.com. The "vow" is a vow for non-violence, a vow for peace.

After visiting this website and understanding the idea, I couldn't take this vow.

Here is why.

For the first thirty-five years of my life, I studied the Bible and participated in evangelical, conservative Christianity. I learned to argue moral and political issues.

When someone said something I disagreed with, I argued.

After all, how could I convince other people they were wrong if I don't argue with them?

What I didn't know at the time was that arguing actually strengthened the opposite point of view because what I focus on expands.

My highly emotional responses of anger and extreme sadness gave extra energy to the moral and political issues of the day. I joined with other people who shared my point of view. We gave the "opposition" so much energy that we began to see supernatural evil forces assisting our opposition.

Everyone we encountered had some kind of "demon" to remove through the power of Jesus. We participated in exorcisms to remove the evil spirits. We did not know we were giving those spirits energy through our rabid opposition.

Our perceptions and interpretations created devils. These devils materialized and inhabited other people. It was a frightening way to live.

That is what we experience during those six months in Greenville, North Carolina as we wrestle with demon-possessed people, casting out demons, renouncing sin, and obsessing in a giddy fascination of power over the supernatural realm.

It climaxes on a spring afternoon when two assistants and I work with a man who says his mother is a witch. He claims she dedicated him to Satan upon his birth.

As we work to cast the demons out of him, the demons use his hands to pin me to the floor by the neck.

I think they will choke me to death. My assistants try to help but the demons are too strong. I imagine the amazing story my death will make. The newspaper headlines will read "Demon-Possessed Man Kills Man During Exorcism."

Then, suddenly, the demon possessed body raises up in the air and gently moves in an arc from the position on top of me to a spot fifteen feet away. There, unseen forces position the man on his back holding his ankles and wrists to the ground as the demons try to lift him from the floor.

With the help of the angels, we finish the exorcism. At the time, I thought we were doing amazing work.

Now, I realize we were using The Law of Attraction to manifest reality from the spiritual realm. We had manifested these beings into our lives to play a role.

Truthfully, my perspective created my demons and I felt an innate need to fight against them.

In addition, over the years, I created other enemies and felt an innate need to fight against them.

As a result, I thought my internal programming might prevent me from keeping the vow for non-violence.

Conspiracy Question

Has there ever been a time in my life when I attempted something and received the exact opposite? Write about that time.

Bonus Material

To learn more about I Take the Vow visit http://itakethevow.com/vow

Chapter 39

There were other reasons I couldn't take the vow.

I love sports. I play as a way to learn how to respond quickly in high-pressure situations.

My recent focus is playing without becoming angry. Some days, I have success. Other days, I don't. Is it possible to play team sports and not be violent?

In addition, was I willing to share the vow with other people?

One of the requirements of the website is that I take the vow and then, share it with at least two other people. Did I really want to do that?

Did I really want to support their vision?

Two days later, I went back to the site.

I went back because the idea wouldn't leave me.

I went back because I read a book that reminded me the Bible records several of Jesus' statements regarding violence. Many of them contradict each other.

However, if we look at the record of Jesus' actions, especially during the crucifixion process, we can see that His actions agree with his teaching in Matthew 5:39 that begin with the phrase "resist not evil…"

I went back because my personal vision is to help others have and maintain Peace of Mind. I know that if enough people have individual peace, World Peace is possible.

The website's vision is my vision.

I became person number 6200 to take the vow. I shared the website with my family.

My wife posted it on her Facebook page.

Almost immediately, a young man responded to her post. I was surprised at what he wrote.

> *Nice thought, but what a bunch of Bologna. To vow non-violence is a good thing, but it will only work if everyone vows it and sticks to it. We all know that this is not going to happen.*
>
> *To say, "Violence is a result of fear and fear is the opposite of Love"...that reminds me of Donnie Darko, and his rebuttal that there are a multitude of emotions besides love and fear.*
>
> *Violence can be spurred from love of your family and knowledge (or you might say fear) of what an enemy will do to them given the chance. So which would be the stronger drive for violence? If there were no love of family, there would be no care for what happened to them and no violence (from you). Would you not agree that it is love in this case that drives violence?*
>
> *Regarding God's "stamp of approval..." God would not put his "stamp of approval" on anyone just because he vows non-violence. Do you believe that every non-violent atheist, Muslim, or Buddhist has God's "stamp of approval"?*
>
> *What of David, who led men in many battles, yet was called a man after Gods own heart? There is more to a person than simply being violent or not. An outward lack of violence tells nothing about a person's heart.*
>
> *World peace? Universal love? Those are two phrases I laugh at. We will not have either until Christ comes back. Is world peace a good goal? Sure it is. Should it be completely ignored? No, but we should not deceive ourselves by pretending that it is something that can be achieved.*
>
> *All of that being said, I respect you for taking the vow of non- violence. I remember watching "The End of the Spear," seeing the missionaries getting killed by natives. One had a gun, but he just shot it in the air,*

> *not at the natives to kill them. He laid down his life allowing the natives to live and learn about Christ. I wonder to myself, would I lay down my life with the knowledge that I am going to heaven rather than take the life of someone unsaved?*

I wasn't surprised because of what he wrote. I know there are many people who believe in enemies and the innate evil of humankind.

I was surprised because he used the same words and examples that I used several years ago to support my justification for violence.

This is significant because it demonstrates how The Law of Attraction works whenever we make a change.

The concept confuses many people. In fact, I did not understand it the first time I heard it explained.

The reason is that, at first glance, this series of events seems to be the opposite of The Law of Attraction. However, it isn't.

The Law of Attractions says attraction happens automatically through the principle of sympathetic vibration. In other words, like attracts like.

That raises the question, "If I take a vow for peace, how do I immediately attract arguments for violence?"

On the surface, it doesn't look as if "like attracts like." It looks as if "like attracts unlike."

There is a reason this happens. It is logical. It changes the way you look at opposition. It allows you to release all your defenses.

> **Conspiracy Question**
>
> What do I feel the need to defend myself against?

Chapter 40

The reason opposites often show up when we attempt to change is that change consists of two steps.

The first step is releasing the old.

The second step is acquiring the new.

When we release the old, we release the associated energy. When we release this energy, it attracts things associated with it.

Therefore, my example, when I take a vow for peace, I release old energy associated with violence and the arguments for violence.

As a result, I attracted those exact arguments.

When this happens, the tendency is to react to it. We usually take it personally.

However, if we really understand this process, there is a more beneficial response.

Steven Covey, author of The Seven Habits of Highly Effective People, says that between an event and its response, there is a pause. This pause is where decisions are made. It may be as long as needed to design the most appropriate response.

When I read the arguments for violence, I know I have to respond so I pause.

I take a day to think about how those arguments are like my old ones. I think about what the young man needs and how The Law of Attraction is working in his life. I think about how when people ask me questions, it is more for my benefit than theirs.

As I formulate my response, I consider the fundamentalist point of view and decide to write so that those with that viewpoint could relate to the response and have to think through my points without completely dismissing them.

My goal is not to oppose the young man. Instead, it was to make him and other readers think.

I know that whenever I oppose something, I give that something energy to hang around longer. I make the release of the old way of thinking difficult.

However, when I observe it and don't react to it, I can release it. It is all part of the process of change.

In addition, I need to go through the process of convincing myself I will take this path and keep the vow.

I decide to respond in a way that is gentle and peaceful. I don't want to give too much energy to his comments. However, I also didn't want to miss the exercise of understanding my internal conflict and resolving it.

Here is what I wrote.

> *Thanks for your comments. I appreciate your thoughts and opinions. I was hesitant to participate in the vow of non-violence. It took me 48 hours to make the decision once I was presented with the opportunity. I hope you don't mind if I share some of my thinking.*
>
> *(I apologize in advance that I don't cover any of these topics in detail. However, I am willing to discuss them here or anywhere else if you want to know more. I take my spirituality seriously and I am always open to considering new ideas when I find that my old ideas lose merit.)*
>
> *As I considered my vow, I had to look at Jesus. (David certainly has merit. However, if we say that his violent actions were after God's heart, we would have to include his adultery, polygamy, and nude dancing in the list of actions too. That discussion is probably better left to another time.)*
>
> *The Bible records several of Jesus' statements regarding violence. Many of them contradict each other so, if we use statements alone, we get a mixed message. However, if we look at the record of Jesus' actions, especially during the crucifixion process, we*

see that His actions agree with his teaching in Matthew 5:39 that start "resist not evil…"

I think this includes protecting loved ones. We can debate the motivation for this protection. My perspective is that the motivation is the fear of losing someone - not love. I don't believe we ever lose someone permanently so there is nothing to be afraid of or protect. If you believe differently, I understand your fears.

I agree that non-violence requires a global commitment, which is why I think this process could work. I don't know that this won't work because my future actions (and everyone else's future actions) do not have to be the same as my previous actions.

The goal of the ITakeTheVow website is one hundred million people. It isn't everybody. It is a good start - and with that many people actively participating, we could see a "tipping point" for world peace - even between the warring religious groups.

Is world peace possible? I believe it is. In fact, the Bible says it is inevitable. "The lion will lay down with the lamb." It just doesn't tell us specifically how it will happen. This could be how it happens. Yes, it is a long shot. Still, wouldn't it be cool if it REALLY DID HAPPEN this way?

I think we are on the threshold of the time for world peace. The Biblical evidence that something significant will happen in the next seven years is overwhelming. (If you don't know what I'm talking about, there is a free ebook available at www.TheReturnOfJesusMyKing.com that explains it.)

In addition, many other religious traditions point to 2012 as a significant year. I don't understand it completely. However, I am convinced something significant will take place.

You asked if I believe every non-violent atheist or

> *Muslim or Buddhist has God's "stamp of approval." My answer is "Yes and more." I believe God created man in God's image. Therefore, every man, woman, and child has God's stamp of approval. It couldn't be otherwise.*

Through this experience, I learn that whenever I step forward to make a major change in my life, opposition must come.

That opposition isn't the devil or Satan or some other evil force. Instead, it is The Law of Attraction at work. The sympathetic vibration from the release of my old energy brings it to me.

My response to this opposition determines whether I successfully make the change.

When I resist it, I focus on the old way of thinking and my change becomes difficult. In fact, the change may not happen.

When I just observe it, see the perfection of it, and understand its purpose, I can truly release the old and move into the new.

In this instance, I have observed it.

I see the perfection of the opposition. It allows me to clarify my intentions.

Now, I am ready to move forward and live a non-violent and peaceful life.

I have Taken the Vow. Will you take it too?

> **Conspiracy Question**
>
> Can I take the vow for Peace/non-violence?
>
> Why or why not?

Chapter 41

One of the amazing things about how life works is that we have the opportunity to learn and relearn until we master a concept.

I learned to focus on love and miracles quite a while ago.

I know that when I practice this, the thing I am opposing goes away. The energy is not re-enforced and it gradually dies.

Those demonic experiences that took place over twenty-five years ago are still fresh in my memory. Because of my perspective at the time, I was certain I was fighting the forces of hell. Now, I know I wasn't.

I was simply manifesting events into my life using The Law of Attraction.

I had an internal conflict between love and hate that manifested in my external life.

Please allow me to explain.

When I focus on love, it expands and hate disappears. When I focus on hate, it expands and love disappears. I cannot love when I hate.

I thought I was loving by fighting the demons. In truth, I was stirring up conflict so I could ride in on my white horse and be the hero.

Today, as my understanding of The Law of Attraction grows, I understand that any conflict I am in is a reflection of an internal conflict. It means I have an error in my perception. It means I am resistant to living within The Law of Miracles and experiencing love.

In the story that opened this book, Kevin tried to hug Pam. However, he pushed her away. He couldn't do both.

It is the same with me. I cannot love when I hate. I cannot accept when I resist.

This gives me guidance for how to respond when I encounter something I don't like. If I oppose and resist it, I give it energy to persist. The vibration continues.

However, when I do not oppose it, the vibration dies. I don't reinforce the situation through high-intensity responses. I experience Peace of Mind in relationships.

This is easy to do through changing my perspective.

I learned this through a personal experience several years ago. In January 1997, I took a position as music director with a local church. My accounting business was thriving and by April of that year, I needed to hire someone to help me. I hired a woman who was part of that group.

As the year went by, our entire family saw this employee as a new family member.

It was normal, natural, and loving.

Much to our surprise, this relationship became a source of gossip, speculation, and eventually, church board meetings.

The leading accuser in this scenario was a family with four children. The mother and father were older than we were. They expressed concern about my marriage and took that concern to the church board. In a period of a year, I sat in three special meetings to address the issue.

To our family, it was much ado about nothing. However, several things came out of this situation.

First, Sheri and I learned deeper communication skills as we talked through the issues.

Second, I watched in surprise as the accusers divorced and divided the church.

Third, I asked the question, "How can a God of love rule by fear?"

It was apparent to me that our family loved our new adopted member. And yet, the church was judging us for it.

Because of my thirty-five plus years of church participation, I knew their speculation and gossip had "circumstantial evidence" and "just cause."

However, the more I thought about it, the more I realized the process had a serious flaw.

God is love. Love is the greatest gift. For God so loved the world... All of these ideas were obvious to me.

And our family was being judged "in the name of love" for loving. The accusers were calling this love sinful.

The contradictions were overwhelming. It took me years to resolve them.

The resolution is obvious. However, society, my religious training, and my lack of security prevented me from acting.

Reconciling these contradictions requires one simple step. All I have to do is change my perspective.

However, when I change my perspective, the ramifications may be radical and audacious.

I will have to evaluate and possibly change life-long belief systems.

I write about my process of changing perspective in the rest of this book.

> **Conspiracy Question**
>
> What disagreements do I currently have with another person?

Chapter 42

Element Two - My Perspective Determines What I See

Perspective is a powerful element in our world. I'm amazed at how often a conversation takes an unexpected turn because of perspective.

In most cases, facts become obsolete. For example, look at this statement.

"Speaking or performing in front of large groups is fun."

Most of you would disagree with me. However, I have pleasant memories of being in front of as many as 52,000 people and enjoying the experience.

You might say, "That's fun for you but not for me." and then tell about the time you panicked and froze while making a presentation.

It is all about perspective. Here is another one.

"The sky is blue."

No, it isn't. Scientists will tell you that the sky isn't blue. The reason we see blue during the day from the perspective of earth is that the air scatters the sunlight and filters out all the other colors.

From our perspective, the sky is blue - even though it really isn't. There are thousands of other examples.

I don't have to list them. It is sufficient to say that the past events in my life create my filter. My filter determines my current perspective.

My perspective is my reality.

When I change my perspective, I change my reality.

There may seem to be many possible life perspectives. However, at the root level, there are only two possible perspectives: duality or unity.

For the first thirty-five years of my life, religion teaches me about a devil. It teaches me about an enemy. As a result, I have the perspective of duality.

This filter influences the way I look at everything. I see good and bad, wrong and right, God and Satan.

I see my business and the competition, my team and the opposition, my philosophy and insanity.

I do not understand that the illusion of duality happens over the truth of unity.

The reason I see so many conflicts is that I have an internal conflict between my ego, my mind, and my spirit. This conflict filters the way I see life.

I see individuals and groups fighting over religion, philosophy, morality, and politics.

This conflict creates drama that occupies much of my life. My perspective is duality and conflict.

I learn about The Law of Attraction. I recognize that the external dramas in my life come from my internal conflicts.

I begin a search to resolve the internal conflicts.

The first step is to discover the source of my internal conflicts.

God programs my spirit before I am born. That is my passion, my Desire. This is my deepest, internal programming. When I live through this Desire, I am "in the flow." This Desire never leaves.

My subconscious mind understands this Desire.

When born into a body, I obtain an ego. My ego interacts with societal influences such as religion, government, and family. These influences add programming to my mind. Some of this programming supports my Desire. However, much of it does not support my Desire.

At the conscious/body/ego level, pleasing society replaces the Desire to follow my passion.

At the Desire/spirit level, the Desire to follow my passion never leaves. At the subconscious/mind level, a conflict rages.

The conflict in my life filters how I see everything around me. I see conflict, war, and struggle.

My life reflects this struggle.

I become conscious of my Desire. However, I move slowly towards my goal because I think life is a struggle.

My perspective is duality and conflict. I learn about filters.

I discover that whenever a person responds to me, it is because of the filter on his or her life.

I discover that whether I see that response as positive or negative is because of the filter on my life.

We use filters in all parts of life.

For example, I use a filter called cable television. We have hundreds of channels that I can access at the push of a button. I don't watch a lot of television but, when I watch it, I want to select exactly what I want to see. I can select from hundreds of channels and, if there is nothing I want to watch there, I can go to the "On Demand" service to watch something archived there. There are hundreds of choices and I filter out all but one through using the remote control to select my channel.

The cable TV analogy opens my understanding of personal filters. Research shows there are thousands of messages sent to my brain every second. These include the sounds I hear, the sights I see, the odors I smell, and the feel of clothing against my skin. In addition, there is the pumping of the blood through my body and the processing of air by my lungs. My filter selects the information I need to recognize just as the remote control selects the channels on my television.

My filter determines how to interpret other people's statements and actions. I evaluate it as praise or criticism. If I determine it is praise, I feel good about myself. I associate that good feeling with the person who made the statement. I decide I like that person.

If I determine it is criticism, I feel bad about myself. I associate that bad feeling with the person who made the statement. I decide I dislike that person.

My filter determines how I interpret the other person's response. More importantly, my filter also determines how the other person responds to me.

The other person only responds to me because I attract that response. My personal resonance attracts that response.

If I feel good about what I do, I receive positive statements. If I feel bad about what I do, I receive negative statements.

If I am not sure how I feel about what I do, I receive both positive and negative statements. In addition, this means I have an internal conflict.

As I said earlier, this internal conflict rages in the mind between my spirit/Desire and my body/ego.

My perspective is duality and conflict.

Over time, I change my filter. I realize that every external conflict I experience represents my internal conflict at the time.

My perspective changes when I integrate my body/ego with my spirit/Desire.

As my filter narrows, I eliminate the illusion of duality. I see the truth of unity.

My perspective changes from duality to unity.

At this point, my entire being vibrates in sympathy with itself.

I integrate all parts of my being for one purpose. I experience "integrity."

Integrity produces the most intense personal energy. It creates peace.

This peace comes as I identify my Desire and bring my entire being into alignment with that Desire. I change my filter to create my perspective of unity.

My perspective of unity allows me to see the same thing in a different way.

As I said earlier, some of this teaching may seem radical. You will find out how radical as you continue reading.

> **Conspiracy Question**
>
> What previous life experience filters the way I see life?

Chapter 43

ELEMENT THREE: I Always Get What I Desire

Before birth, God programs my spirit with my Desire.

During childhood, society programs my body/ego to please others. The conflict between my sprit and body plays out in my subconscious/mind.

Once I understand this, I decide to change perspective from duality to unity so that my entire being may resonate with my Desire. This is integrity because I integrate all parts of my being to accomplish my Desire.

Integrity has many benefits.

When I experience integrity, I can listen to my feelings and determine if what I am doing is what I Desire. Moving closer to my Desire resonates within my being and my joy increases. Moving away from my Desire interferes with my internal vibration and creates strife.

When I experience integrity, it is easier to build relationships because other people feel my confidence. They sense my positive vibration.

When I try to please the people around me, I am out of integrity. This confuses other people because my frequency is always changing.

This makes communication difficult at best, impossible at worst. My relationships suffer.

When I initially decide to change my perspective from duality to unity, I think the battle is between my conscious and subconscious. I spend great energy attempting to reprogram my mind.

The problem with this way of thinking is that it is still duality.

The battles still rages. I still experience conflict with those around me. I attempt to resolve this conflict.

With my perspective of duality, I see conflict and resolution as a normal part of life.

Art, literature, music, math, science, politics, and many other topics use conflict and resolution as a crucial element. At least that is my perception.

I think conflict and resolution come from change.

I'm not the only one. Much of our Western civilization believes this. I fight to maintain integrity. This struggle persists. I feel separated from my Desire.

I believe that society is conspiring against me. I talk about unity. I explain unity.

I live in duality.

Then, one quote changes my perspective.

> *"It may seem like luck. It is not. The truth is that life is conspiring in your favor. It may not look that way at the time. However, everything that happens brings you closer to that which you Desire."*

I realize that even my opposition brings me closer to what I Desire. When I see my opposition as God's hands bringing me my Desire, my perspective changes.

I understand that my conflicts do not come from change. Change is a normal part of life.

However, I resist change because I think change requires internal conflict and resolution.

When I have internal conflict, I attract external conflicts. The only way to resolve the external conflicts is to resolve the internal ones.

I recognize that change is normal. It is healthy. It is growth. Life must have change to exist.

My conflicts come from my perspective of duality.

When I change my perspective to unity, conflict disappears. My Desire, given to me by God must come to me.

God decrees it. I decree it.

The Universe works in harmony to bring it to me.

I discover that the key to receiving the maximum benefit from the Law of Attraction and receiving my Desire is changing perspective.

With the perspective of duality, everything opposes me.

With the perspective of unity, nothing opposes me. Everything works on my behalf to bring me what I Desire.

> **Conspiracy Question**
>
> What does "Life is a Conspiracy for Me" mean to me?
>
> Whom do I trust the least?
>
> What benefit do I receive from my relationship with this person?
>
> How can I demonstrate love to this person?

Chapter 44

Once I discover that I can easily get what I Desire if I establish and maintain a perspective of unity, I program my subconscious for this. This is helpful.

It removes old programming and brings me closer to Desire. This enacts The Law of Attraction by using sympathetic vibration to manifest what I Desire.

My perspective of unity brings love. This enacts The Law of Miracles. The Law of Miracles allows me to experience shortcuts in time and space.

I learn that to truly experience love, I must see others as myself and myself as others.

I know that, by definition, seeing others as myself is unity.

This makes sense to me. Love is unity. Unity is love. However, this concept feels vague.

Therefore, in an attempt to identify the details of it, I attempt to list what love/unity looks like.

I determine that a life of love and unity is a life without resistance. It is a life without defense.

In fact, when I defend myself, I block the voice of God from speaking to me.

Any type of resistance resists everything.

If I put defense around me, I prevent my Desire from coming true. Let's talk about defense for a minute.

I have a client who is a self-defense instructor. He has guns, knives, sticks, and all kinds of weapons. They are in his car, his house, everywhere he is. More than once, we've started a meeting by him unloading his pistol.

He requires other people to earn his trust and once earned, it can be quickly lost. He often changes seats in public if someone sits directly behind him.

Because he is always in a defensive mode, he always has attacks coming to him. I can't tell you how many times he has encountered an attack of some type during the brief time I've known him. The attacks come in the form of volatile relationship, vehicle accidents, and failed business relationships.

He responds by putting up more measures that are defensive. Me, on the other hand, I'm learning to let my defenses down.

I know that if I lock myself away from others, I lock out blessings.

My greatest insight on this topic comes in the summer of 2006.

We have friends who own a section of the Pecos River that winds through a box canyon. We spend several weekends there that summer. The privacy and seclusion attracts us just as it attracted explorers in the 1600s and United States Presidents in the 1900s.

They have since sold much of the land. However, we enjoy it during that summer and visit on numerous occasions.

On one visit, the shallow river runs past my feet and lower legs as I walk down the river. The water, fed by the summer snowmelt, is cold. It is so cold that I need the summer sun on the top half of my body to keep me from shivering as I walk through the water. My intention is to skinny dip but the river isn't deep enough today.

Since I can't truly skinny dip, I decide to do something I've never done before, wade through the water sans clothes. I'm in a private area of the river but not so private that a visitor or two might not arrive. I throw caution to the wind and my shorts on the shore. I'll get them when I return.

My motivation for trying the new experience is nothing more than the thrill of something new and naughty. However, I am about to discover something deeper.

I grew up in a conservative, religious environment. My family, my church, my school, and my community had similar beliefs. Those beliefs covered many topics. One of those topics was nudity. The message to me was very clear. "Nudity is wrong."

There are three exceptions (and no more):

1. A doctor can see a nude person because that's his job. (Children in my neighborhood often played doctor so we could see each other nude. We conducted the activity in a purely professional playtime until our parents caught wind of it and made us stop.)

2. A married couple can see each other nude. (However, some couples don't want to do that.)

3. A baby can be seen nude. (That's the only way to change its diaper.)

High school and college were more of the same. Classes taught me the inappropriateness of nudity. If a liberal professor opened the door to new ideas on the topic, my classmates and I quickly slammed it shut.

When I married my wife, we discussed nudity. We decided we were OK with it around each other but we didn't want to be nude around our kids. (See exception number 2.)

When our children were born, we used exception number 3 to change their diapers. However, once our children were old enough, we stressed the importance of clothing to cover the body. We taught them what we were taught.

In spite of these teachings to the contrary, I find myself, in the summer of 2006, deciding to take a nude walk down the Pecos River. This action certainly did not fit within any of the three exceptions.

I noticed during a previous visit that some of my family had discreetly found a place to skinny dip. I didn't participate. My excuse was "The water is too cold."

The river is lower by the time we make our next visit so a nude walk in the water is the best I can do. I am grateful for that because the water is still very cold.

The geography makes it almost impossible for someone to see me so there isn't much risk. Still, I feel vulnerable.

As I enjoy the water and the scenery, something significant happens deep within me. I don't understand it but I know it is there.

I experience nature without barriers. I sense new freedom. I feel a greater awareness of love deep within me. I feel it but I can't completely put it into words.

I decide to walk nude again the next day and see if I can figure it out.

Conspiracy Question

What causes me to feel naked/vulnerable?

Chapter 45

Between my walks in the river, I read a book by Deepak Chopra. It may seem like a random coincidence to you. However, I assure you, it was not. I attracted this book into my life.

The title of the book is *The Spontaneous Fulfillment of Desire – Harnessing the Infinite Power of Coincidence*.

In it, he observes that a divine force connects the universe. It is apparent in everything – especially nature.

He uses the examples of birds in flocks and fish in schools. Here are his words.

> *"They all seem to be moving in formation. When they change direction, they all execute the same motions synchronistically.*
>
> *A single school of fish can include hundreds of individuals, yet each fish moves in harmony with every other fish without an obvious leader. They change direction in an instant, all fish altering their course at the exact same moment, and they do it perfectly. You never see fish bumping into each other as they swim. They look like a single organism as if some unspoken command was issued that they all obeyed at once. How is that happening? There is not enough time for any exchange of information, so any correlation of activity among the fish must be happening non-locally.*
>
> *The instantaneous communication we commonly see in schools of fish comes from the spiritual level, the organizing nonlocal intelligence in the virtual domain. The result is synchronicity, beings that are totally in tune with their environment and with each other, dancing to the rhythm of the cosmos."*

The next day, as I again walk nude through the Pecos River, I notice pools full of trout fingerlings. Every time I approach a pool, I see examples of how the fish move as a single organism. The trout move in perfect sync with one another in response to my presence.

This doesn't surprise me. I've seen it many times before. Fish do it. Birds do it. It is evident in many examples of nature. However, I had never considered those movements as evidence of a divine source orchestrating the events.

If this is true for birds and fish, it must be true for the events in my life too, including my relationships. Is it possible that the resistance I carry is the only reason I don't see the orchestration in my life as obviously as I see it in the lives of fish and birds?

Over the next several weeks, I think about my experience. I share it with my friends. Responses range from surprise to horror. I hear questions like, "Weren't you afraid someone would see you?", "Did you get sunburned?", and "Who went with you?" No one provides insight to my spiritual feelings. My friends are too shocked about my "outrageous action" to consider the deeper significance.

I think more about my experience. I use it as a focus for my meditation. My reading takes me through a passage in Volume 2 of *Conversation with God* written by Neale Donald Walsch. The topic is visibility. The author talks with God about visibility in relationships, visibility in business, and visibility in government.

This isn't the type of visibility where we promote ourselves through advertising, smooth talk and public service announcements. It is the type where everything we do is visible to others. They see us. They see our motives. They see who we really are. There are no secrets.

As I read the book's dialogue, I realize the ramifications of visibility are tremendous. Friends learn to trust us. Customers know our costs and recognize the fairness in our pricing. Governments negotiate in good faith. There are no secrets.

As the dialogue continues, the topic evolves from visibility to nakedness. God and Mr. Walsch assume that lovers are comfortable being physically naked in front of each other but, what about emotional nakedness? Can married partners, lovers, and life partners experience emotional nakedness with one another?

The author, who has experienced several divorces, concludes that emotional nakedness is much more difficult than physical nakedness.

God agrees and challenges him to be a catalyst to change the world. God literally dares Neale Donald Walsch to change the world through the concept of emotional nakedness.

I understand that challenge because, at that moment, I gain understanding of what I felt when I walked in the river. Physical nakedness is an object lesson for emotional nakedness. That's what I felt in the river. That's why I felt love. The removal of clothing barriers led to the removal of emotional barriers.

I decide to do further research on this topic. I discover there are some benefits to physical nakedness.

- Benjamin Franklin made an "air bath" part of his daily routine. He believed it was essential to maintaining good health.

- Recent medical studies show that 20-30 minutes of daily sun exposure to at least eighty-five percent of the body prevents cancer.

I discover the benefits to emotional nakedness are greater.

Our modern society teaches us to cover feelings. The common opinion is that it is OK to feel as long as that feeling isn't expressed in a way that makes others uncomfortable.

We become afraid of what others think. It is such an ingrained part of our lifestyle that we take it for granted. This produces communication problems. We want other people to understand us but we don't give them enough information to understand us.

Businesses, families, and friendships suffer damage because of assumptions, lack of communication, and lies.

On the other hand, emotional nakedness means there are no secrets. We share our feelings. We talk about our hurts. We work through situations with no hidden agendas. The flow of conversations and feelings is refreshing and pure, just like the cold water rushing over my legs on a summer day.

This truth resonates within me. There is more here that I need to know. I research nudist societies. I had previously seen nudists as leftovers from the hippy movement of the 1960s. I assumed they were drug users and free lovers with no sense of accountability or morals. Is it possible they have more emotional maturity than the rest of society?

I see hints of emotional openness in their websites but most of their information talks about the physical benefits of nudity. I understood their points but they seem shallow. I know there is more to this topic.

I'm an avid reader. I read several magazines and one to two books a week. I often put several books on hold at the local library and read each as it becomes available. I notice that each book falls into my hands when I need it.

At this time, the book that becomes available is Marlo Morgan's *Mutant Message Down Under*. In it, she writes about her experience with an Australian Aborigine tribe. The story paints vivid pictures of a misunderstood people.

This is my first time reading about Aborigines. I previously considered them a group of uncivilized savages. As I read Mutant, I learn they see human beings as fully spiritual beings. However, they believe emotional coverings turn humans from spiritual beings into mutants.

The book contains many rich insights about life. The following six intrigue me the most.

1. The Aborigines have no secrets among themselves so they do not wear clothing.
2. The absence of secrets and the willingness to share openly means there is no need to talk to communicate. Communication takes place via telepathy.
3. This communication is not limited to humans. It also takes place with plants and animals.
4. The Aborigines believe all humans have this capability.
5. The Aborigines believe humans lose this capability when we hide things from one another.
6. This hiding turns human beings into mutants.

The message of the book is clear. Human beings mutate our spiritual abilities by covering our feelings, our thoughts, and our bodies. I wonder if the simple uncovering of my body while visiting the river began turning me from a "mutant" into a human again.

I share this information with my family and we discuss nudity. The discussion is simple. Everyone has the opportunity to talk about his or her feelings on the subject. Some state they are ready to participate immediately. Others want to participate but they need time to redo their programming. (Remember, we had taught them the importance of clothing when they were younger.) Everyone agrees that they don't mind other people's nudity.

We discuss nude etiquette (always sit on a towel). We agree to communicate clearly regarding visitors so there are no surprises. We decide to see what happens because of our new understandings.

Initially, there isn't much nudity practiced outside of the hot tub and the privacy of our own bedrooms. However, as time goes by, we each become more comfortable with wearing less clothing.

Then, the remarkable starts to happen.

We discover that the ability to remove clothing makes it easier to remove the barriers in other parts of our lives too. Our children begin to talk to us about a long-standing problem with their home schooling. An older child talks about a new experience he had previously been unwilling to share. New business opportunities fall into our laps.

Is there a connection between nakedness and the remarkable happenings?

Conspiracy Question

Am I comfortable being physically naked with anyone in my life?

Who?

Would I be comfortable being physically naked with everyone in my life?

Why or why not?

Am I comfortable being emotionally naked with anyone in my life?

Who?

Would I be comfortable being emotionally naked with everyone in my life?

Why or why not?

Chapter 46

The greatest obstacle to taking action is fear. We are afraid of what others will think when we do something. We are afraid of the results. We are afraid of failure. In summary, we are afraid of exposure.

Exposure is one of our greatest fears. You can probably think of something in your past that very few people know about you. You may be afraid that if your family members, your co-workers, or your friends learn about this, you will suffer harm. If you believe in a judgment after death, the fear of exposure contributes to a fear of death where "everything will be revealed."

My observation is that the fear of the exposure of those past events correlates to the fear of the exposure of the body.

It is the same paralyzing fear.

It prevents you from serving others because you remember how politicians are "destroyed" by the media for similar actions. It prevents you from pursuing your dreams because, if you become famous, your life becomes an open book. It prevents you from pursuing a relationship because you think the other person won't like you when they discover the truth.

This fear holds power over you and prevents action.

This fear held power over us and prevented us from acting. However, as we experienced physical nakedness, that fear left. The action of removing clothing gave us the courage to take other actions. Removing physical barriers leads to the removal of
emotional barriers. As a result, conversations opened and new opportunities initiated themselves.

Physical nakedness led to emotional nakedness.

Physical nakedness was a catalyst to completely trusting everyone in my life. However, the removal of barriers didn't stop there.

Other barriers came down too including barriers to love.

Conspiracy Question

What current situation harms me the most?

What benefit do I receive from this situation?

Chapter 47

The insight about nakedness may seem radical to you.

However, this chapter contains insights that may appear even more radical to you.

Before I continue, I remind you that one of the characteristics of Living the Southwest Lifestyle is Integrity. I define that as spiritual understanding without exceptions

Spiritual understanding applied to all areas of life, without exceptions, appears radical because it is not something most people do. The result is a lack of integrity that produces struggle and suffering.

It is my opinion that the cause of all struggle and suffering in our western society comes from a lack of integrity in our current system of love.

Love functions through giving and receiving. We give love to other people.
We receive love from other people.

This requires freedom and no defenses.

However, our society uses a system that is comparable to slavery. People own each other. We use the terms "my wife," "my husband," and "my lover."

This system uses religion and legal contracts to confirm and establish love relationships.

As one comedian puts it, "This relationship that I have with you is so special that I must get the church and government in on it."

These contracts and agreements protect the parties. We call it marriage.

We take it further to the family structure.

We establish "parental rights" as a legal way of establishing ownership of our children and use the terms "my son," "my daughter," and "my child."

We think that, by setting up defense systems, the parties can't get hurt.

It is so ingrained into our system, that same-sex couples want the "benefits" of the marriage laws.

My question is "how is that working for us?"

A few years ago, divorce rates were at an all-time high. That rate has come down recently.

That doesn't mean more marriages are lasting. It means more marriages aren't happening, except for the states where same-sex marriages are now legal.

Don't get me wrong. I'm not against marriage. I'm not against the family. I'm just pointing out why they often struggle and produce suffering.

Marriages are relationships. Relationships need agreements to function.

Once two parties make an agreement, the agreement becomes part of the past.

Past agreements don't always work in the present.

The reason is that perspective changes. We don't see things the same way.

Agreements must have room for flexibility and current marriage agreements don't allow for that.

According to marriage agreements, one person owns another. This feels secure because it is in the past. The past is secure because we believe it can't change.

However, the present is not secure. The current moment, the present, is limitless. The reason is that it exists of pure potential.

Pure potential does not feel secure because anything can happen. It truly is limitless.

As I realize this, it becomes apparent to me that man created the concept of marriage to control his female property and his offspring.

Marriage laws use fear of loss to keep a love relationship together. Anyone who goes through a divorce quickly understands that it isn't about love. Love is just a sideshow.

Marriage and divorce laws are about ownership of people, places, and things.

They are the perfect representation of a God of love ruling by fear. And, if a God of love can't rule by fear, then marriage laws can't enforce love by fear either.

As I explored this spiritual truth without exceptions, I had to rethink marriage.

Marriage, as it exists, is slavery. It is ownership of another person. It is love enforced by a contract. It is love governed by fear.

I am not judging married people. I am still married. I supported my daughter when she chose to get married. I support and encourage others who wish to enter into a marriage agreement.

I am saying that the marriage laws, as they currently exist, are an example of enforcing love with fear.

Whenever we enforce love with fear, we produce struggle and suffering. This erects barriers to love. Our society, our religion, and our lack of security claim we are so incapable of true love, that we must enforce our love relationships with fear.

However, when we allow love to exist without fear, when we remove the barriers to love, when we recognize all of us are connected in unity, there are many benefits.

Conspiracy Questions

What agreement have I made in the past that I was not able to keep?

Did the fear of loss prevent me from breaking the agreement?

What agreement have I made with someone in the past that the other party was not able to keep?

Did the fear of loss prevent the other party from breaking the agreement?

What agreements have I made in the past that I completely kept?

Why are agreements so difficult to keep?

Chapter 48

Once I understand that marriage laws are a defensive mechanism to protect me from loss, I have to rethink the entire concept.

There are benefits to marriage. However, they are limiting.

When we remove the barriers created by marriage laws, this opens the door to pure potential. One part of this potential is multiple love relationships. When I first recognized this, I didn't know what to do with it.

Sheri and I discuss it. We admit to one another that we love other people in our lives. However, we do not act on that love because we are afraid of what we will lose if we do.

We agree that we like our relationship, our family, and our life together. However, we also recognize that the freedom to love all is in integrity with God being love.

In addition, we discuss how the freedom to love others without the fear of loss would improve the quality of our lives.

We decide to explore other love relationships.

Even though we have explored this lifestyle since the late 1990s, we didn't know what to call this until the spring of 2008. At that time, we discovered an article on something called "Polyamory." By definition, it means, "The love of many."

(Wikipedia (www.wikipedia.com) has a lengthy article about it so I refer you there if you want to know more.)

In short, Polyamory isn't swinging in the sense that it is about sex. Sex may or may not be a part of it.

Polyamory is about building relationships without limits.

For most of us, this is the last line of defense in trusting everyone, in being completely naked.

In addition, for most of us, we may not be ready to drop this last line of defense.

However, I believe it is in congruent with the perspective of unity presented in this book.

Polyamory is not a new concept. Islam, Judaism and Christianity have their roots in the polyamorous triad of Abraham, Hagar and Sarah.

There are societies that practice multiple partners. In some societies, men collect wives as property. I'm not talking about that. I'm talking about societies where there is a sense of unity and love.

Our civilization might call these savage cultures.

If so, we may need to reconsider our perspective of these cultures – especially in light of the following story.

I recently asked a Native American teacher if the system of his ancestors was patriarchal or matriarchal. The answer I received surprised me.

> *"It was neither. It was matrilineal. This system was used in most tribes prior to the white man's teaching of personal ownership of other people through marriage.*
>
> *The women had the final say but there wasn't one woman in charge, they ruled by committee.*
>
> *At that time, there was community. There was shared love. The women led because they had the power of life. The women chose their sexual partners and, when they chose multiple partners, there was uncertainty as to the identity of the father.*
>
> *In our society, we would worry about the paternal responsibility for the offspring. Which child should a man love and provide for if he didn't know which child was his?*
>
> *This was never an issue in the tribe. The reason is that every man loved all the children because he assumed he had the responsibility for all of them."*

I sat in silence. Can it be that simple?

It is. His story describes the perspective of unity I describe in this book.

Because, in truth, that is the way it is. We each have a responsibility to one another for care, love, and provision.

When I equate love with ownership, I lay the foundation for envy, jealousy, and rivalry. It creates barriers and I attract those things info my life. This causes pain and struggle as I pursue my Desire
When I equate love with unity with the world around me, I attract love and unity into my life. This brings Peace of Mind as I pursue my Desire.

Everything in my life moves me toward my ultimate Desire. It is up to me to decide if I want to go there painfully or Peacefully.

Either way, it is a conspiracy for me

The same process that worked to bring Sheri and me together in 1985, works to bring everything into our lives to fulfill our Desire.

Sympathetic vibration makes it happen. If we block that energy, we struggle through the process.

When we drop all defenses, we expedite the process.

I believe that you and I are like those fish. As we move individually towards accomplishing our individual Desires, we move cooperatively to accomplish a greater Desire.

In many cases, those Desires overlap. For example, Sheri and I have similar Desires. We cannot fulfill them alone.

In the Personal Peace section of the book, I told you the story of my friend's house that burnt down. My son, Peter saw a vision of a valuable ring in the ashes. However, he couldn't find it there.

As a result, he didn't tell anyone.

One of our friends went there to look a day or so later and she found the ring in the exact same spot Peter saw. I believe their connection allowed her to see what he saw.

That connection allowed them to fulfill the Desire of finding the precious ring for our friend.

In the same way, you and I are connected to one another. We are all connected to each other, to everything, and to God.

The reason we don't feel that connection is that we are defensive. We have barriers that hinder the connection.

However, when the defenses drop, when we become naked, when we truly love all without hesitancy, we experience the Law of Attraction without barriers.

We experience Relationship Peace of Mind.

> **Conspiracy Question**
>
> What defense mechanism can I drop today?

Chapter 49

More Information on Nakedness

I had no idea what would happen when I stepped into the river on that summer day and removed my clothing. Looking back, I see that simple act led to a world of unprecedented change in my life. The fear of exposure washed down the river, never to return.

Are you ready for that change? Are you ready to become vulnerable? Are you ready to experience a life without physical and emotional barriers?

If you are, I invite you to explore a life without barriers and tell us about your experiences through using the contact information on the back of this book.

If you still have questions, this list contains the most commonly asked questions about physical and emotional nakedness.

I see that nakedness is valuable but I'm not sure what to do next. How do I start practicing this in my life?

Experiment privately first by being nude in a place or activity where you have not been nude before. Suggestions include the hot tub, swimming, and sunbathing.

I've done those things. The challenge for me is living nude. How can I do that?

The easiest way is to start. If you prefer to do things slowly, rather than all at once, start by wearing less clothing than you normally would.

I live with other people. How do I start this?

Talk to them. Remember, the goal is to use physical nakedness as a tool to explore emotional nakedness. Our family discussions about physical nakedness created an atmosphere where emotional nakedness could take place without judgment. If you have trouble starting the conversation, invite them to participate in a Living Southwest Lifestyle Relationship Peace of Mind Seminar.

How do I respond if the people I live with are opposed to nudity?

There are numerous reasons for opposition to nudity. They include religious teaching, embarrassment, and previous emotional or sexual abuse. It may be appropriate to ask questions to reveal the source of this opposition. Please note that this should be done very gently and without judgment. Many people are not consciously aware of the source of their opposition because they acquired it over many years. The purpose of the questioning is to help identify the sources of the opposition.

If it is not appropriate to ask those questions, then I suggest you talk about your Desires and determine what everyone is comfortable with before proceeding.

Is nudity legal?

Most communities have laws against public nudity. However, it is legal to be nude in a private environment.

Is there a special etiquette for nudity?

Yes, carry a towel to sit on. Otherwise, just use common sense and good manners.

How should I discuss this topic with my children?

I talk with my children regarding any topic the same way as I talk with adults. This removes the taboo and allows them to know they can talk to me about any subject.

Will the experience of physical nakedness automatically produce emotional nakedness?

No, emotional nakedness does not happen automatically. I find that it is easier to be physically naked than it is to be emotionally naked. The reason is that if I am not 100% comfortable being physically naked in front of someone, there is something about me I want to hide from them.

If I trust someone enough to be physically naked with him or her, I may trust that person enough to be emotionally naked also. However, if I'm not comfortable being physically naked with someone, I won't be comfortable being emotionally naked with him or her either.

How do I become comfortable with emotional nakedness?

The first step for me is physical nakedness. I use it as a "measuring stick" for emotional nakedness. For example, if I have a meeting scheduled with someone, I ask myself if I would be comfortable meeting with them naked. If the answer is "yes," I know I can be emotionally naked with them. However, if the answer is "no," I look closer to see why I don't trust that person.

Of course, I don't conduct business meetings nude. However, the exercise gives me a valuable tool I can use to measure the level of openness I feel with that person.

I agree that emotional nakedness is more difficult than physical nakedness. I have something in my past that I have kept from my family. How do you suggest I handle that?

The "something in your past" is less important than how you feel about it. If you are afraid of someone finding out about it, that fear prevents you from being open in your relationships. I believe that tactful communication about this event is the first step.

I am afraid of other people's responses if they find out about this thing from my past. How do I get over that fear?

People who love you may already sense your past so they may not be

surprised. The worst that can happen is that the relationship changes form. My experience is that it is always best to share the information at an appropriate time. The trust this establishes outweighs the potential negative response. More often than not,
this improves the relationship.

I think the risk is too great. I'm afraid I'll lose this relationship.

If the truth of the past causes you to lose the relationships, the other person does not love all of you, he or she only loves a part of you. When you keep secrets from the one closest to you, you literally cut off a part of yourself from that person. This means he or she doesn't know all of you. This incompleteness prevents the relationship from being all it could be.

Why is this so important to you?

One of my goals is to love and trust each person in my life. Emotional nakedness and physical nakedness are the most accurate tools I have found for determining how I'm doing with this goal.

Financial Peace of Mind

*How to Live Within
The Law of Abundance*

Chapter 50

"Do not go in. I repeat. Do not go in."

The voice on Robert's radio is his commanding officer. Americans are under ambush in the jungles of Vietnam.

Robert, as an American helicopter pilot, has just radioed that he is going in to help.

His commanding officer thinks the situation is too hot to risk additional American assets and he overrules Robert's intention.

Robert ignores the commanding officer. He decides to tell him he didn't hear the transmission. He flies into the middle of the firefight and...

Well, I'm getting ahead of myself. I will tell you the rest of this remarkable story later. It is a story of abundance, gratitude, and generosity. It is a story of living in the moment. It demonstrates that no matter what you're facing, the solution is the same. It is simple.
It is glorious. It is fulfilling.

And, I fully promise that, no matter how difficult your financial situation is, that even if you think you have never experienced more than an iota of prosperity, that even if you have a stack of unpaid bills at home and are on the edge of bankruptcy, this material will bring you Peace of Mind in your finances.

By the time you finish this book, you will understand how The Law of Abundance works and how you can use it in your life.

You will be able to use this material to build an abundant life. However, you will only be able to do this IF you Desire to do so.

Before I go further, I need to explain that if you don't currently experience abundance in your life, this teaching may seem radical.

It may rub you the wrong way. It may make you dreadfully uncomfortable.

Throughout the rest of this book, I share deeply personal stories. I may challenge your life-long convictions.

Just remember this. The results in your life came from what you did in the past. If you don't like what you have now, you must do something differently to get different results.

Robert did that. In fact, it was remarkable that Robert was even in Vietnam.

A short time earlier, he was in San Francisco's Haight Ashbury neighborhood protesting the Vietnam War. He didn't leave his heart in San Francisco. However, I suspect he may have found at least a part of it there.

While protesting the war in the late 1960s, he begins to ask questions. Why is he protesting the war? What is the war about? He can't answer those questions. His fellow protestors can't either so he decides to find out for himself by enlisting.

You can imagine his parents' surprise when he calls to tell them he is coming home from protesting the war to go fight in it. He hitchhikes from San Francisco back to New Mexico and visits the Santa Fe recruiting office.

He requests flight training. The recruiter thinks it is odd that a war protestor now wants to participate in the war. After quite a bit of convincing, Robert receives admission to flight school with the condition that if he makes one mistake, he will go to ground force training and not receive credit for any time spent in flight school.

Robert finishes flight training without making that mistake and goes to Vietnam in 1970 as a pilot of a helicopter gun ship. His responsibilities include leaving for a mission within moments of receiving the orders. He does this day or night, with or without sleep. He and his fellow pilots discover that the best way to do this at night is to sleep in the choppers.

It was during one of these missions that he hears that call for help, radios that he is going in to help, ignores his commanding officer's orders not to go in, and flies into the middle of the firefight.

He finds the Americans, picks them up, flies them to safety, and drops them off. As the leader of these rescued men exits the chopper, he leans in to see the name on Robert's flight jacket and tells him, "I'll never forget you and if I can ever do anything for you, just name it."

As far as Robert is concerned, this man is a mercenary, under the radar and outside the law. He is a soldier of fortune operating in the interest of the United States.

He has government support. However, if he ever makes a mistake, the government will completely deny his existence.

Later in his life, Robert is grateful to have that man's promise.

> **Conspiracy Question**
>
> Do I feel like I live an abundant life?
>
> Why or why not?

Chapter 51

In the early 1970s, I am just entering puberty. I remember playing Dixie Youth baseball and I remember watching our old black and white TV as the boats full of evacuees leave Vietnam before the Communists take over the country. I remember being sad that the greatest nation in the world, my nation, has lost its first war.

Today, I still don't understand what happened in Vietnam. However, I remember all of those people jammed into those ships leaving the country. I remember how our country opened our borders to those people who managed to leave.

One of those people is a little child, the only member of the family who is able to board.

Somehow, this ten-year-old boy gets on a boat, comes across the ocean, and arrives in the United States. When he arrives, he goes through the system and a family adopts him into the most prosperous country on earth in the twentieth century.

The abundance of the United States is a mystery to those who come to visit. Many other countries practice poverty, even though abundance surrounds them.

There are parts of the United States where we practice poverty too. However, for this young person and his new family, there is enough supply for them to come together and start a new life.

I can identify with that.

If you have read my other books or heard me speak, you may know the story of what happened to me in the summer of 1984.

I attend a seminar in the Baltimore, Maryland Civic Center. As I listen to the material, a Desire grows within me. It impresses me. It excites me. It emotionally charges me.

More than twenty years later, this Desire is still with me. It is a driving, compelling Desire. It is the Desire of creating a family of fifty people in three generations to make the world a better place.

I meet my future wife, Sheri, in the fall of 1984. She has a similar Desire and decides to join me during the spring of 1985. We marry on January 1, 1986.

With step one accomplished, we move to step two - have children. Since our goal is to have eight children, we determine that time is of the essence and we do what newlyweds do. We start the reproduction process.

We expect to have our first child by our first anniversary. Two months go by and Sheri is not pregnant. Two months become five, and five months become seven.

We wonder if we're doing it right. We hear stories of couples becoming pregnant while using birth control. We aren't using birth control and we aren't pregnant. We won't have a child by our first anniversary.

However, on August 1, after seven full months of marriage, Sheri discovers she is pregnant. We are thrilled beyond measure. We are on our way.

By November, the doctors think something is amiss and they schedule an ultrasound for Thanksgiving week. My parents are visiting for the holiday and they join us at the doctor's office.

There is tension in the room as the doctor starts the procedure by putting gel on Sheri's stomach. The gel is a conductor for sound waves.

Next, he uses a transducer to send sound waves into the uterus. The sound waves bounce off bones and tissue returning back to the transducer to generate black and white images. We are using technology to see inside Sheri's body.

The doctor looks on the screen to confirm his suspicions. We look with him as he carefully explains what we see. He points to something on the right side of Sheri's abdomen and says, "There is the baby."

Then, he points to something on the left side of her abdomen and says, "There is the other baby."

We are having twins. Both babies are healthy and normal. We

celebrate Thanksgiving with tremendous enthusiasm.

I don't have a name for it at the time. However, I know we are experiencing something profound. I know today that it was the Law of Abundance at work.

The Law of Abundance states everything reproduces through multiplication over time to produce resources sufficient for all Desire.

Some people believe in the Law of Abundance. Others believe in scarcity or lack.
When I first share my vision of creating a family of fifty people in three generations to make a positive impact on the world, I discover that most of my friends believe in scarcity.

They oppose my abundant vision. They doubt me when I start talking about it. When Sheri and I marry, they take me aside and say it is unfair to ask her to have eight children.

Then, they said we cannot afford to have eight children and teach them at home.

On the other hand, a few of my friends believe in abundance. They see the demonstrations of this law in our daily lives. They understand that lack is always temporary and that nature is infinitely abundant.

Their abundant attitudes encourage us as we start towards the fulfillment of our vision. Their generosity paves the way for us to take the next step.

There are three elements in The Law of Abundance. They are:

1. Abundance is a Normal Act of Nature
2. Lack is Always Temporary
3. Gratefulness Accelerates the Law of Abundance

> **Conspiracy Question**
>
> Do I live my life with an attitude of abundance or an attitude of lack?

Chapter 52

ELEMENT ONE: Abundance is a Normal Act of Nature

The design of nature is reproduction through multiplication. One seed of corn planted, grown, and cared for produces an infinite amount of corn.

This is true throughout nature. Let's look at some examples from the Southwestern United States.

Tumbleweeds are a huge part of the Southwestern landscape. We have so many in New Mexico that we make snowmen out of them during the holiday season.

Did you know that real name of the plant is "Russian Thistle" and that tumbleweed did not appear in the United States until 1877?

The first recorded tumbleweed was in South Dakota in 1877. By 1900, tumbleweed spread to the Pacific coast.

It is so abundant that most people think it has always been part of our Western landscape.

There are no limits to the number of offspring produced by anything in nature.

Our family lives in a high mountain desert valley. There are examples of abundance all around us. The juniper trees and cactus grow easily. We see flowering plants every spring, summer, and fall. The birds and wildlife are everywhere.

As I write this material, I only have to turn my head and look out the window to see an assortment of doves, finches, towhees, blue jays, and sparrows. By the time each day is over, I see rabbits, quail, crows, vultures, hawks and a surprise or two like a cedar waxwing, grosbeak, or red-winged blackbird. During the summer, more than fifty hummingbirds visit our feeders daily.

Abundance is strong and vibrant in nature. It overcomes many obstacles.

We live on a rural road. It was a dirt road until just a few years ago. Then, the county covered the dirt with asphalt. A few months after the asphalt project was complete, we took an evening walk.

Imagine our surprise when we noticed plants growing through the asphalt. That's right, the asphalt had been laid down and compressed on top of those plants but that didn't stop them. They grew right through it. That is the Law of Abundance at work.

The valley we live in is located east of the Sandia Mountains. These mountains are a study in contrasts. The reasons for the contrasts are climatic. The winds are normally from the west.

The west side of the Sandias receives the brunt of those winds. They serve as a counter measure against any moisture that may wonder into the area. After the winds hit the west side of the mountain, they go up and over the mountain to blow across the plains of eastern New Mexico. The mountain protects our little valley from the strongest winds.

When cooler Canadian air comes into the area from the north, it moves down the east side of the Sandias. The mountain range traps it there. This cooler air wrings out any moisture coming over the mountain. If the Canadian cold front is especially strong, it will hold the moisture against the mountain for a day or two but not push the moisture over the mountain. As a result, the east side of the mountains receives twice the rainfall as the west side.

I have lived in that valley since 1987 and I'm amazed at how the mountain is so different on one side than the other.

The west side of the mountain is pure desert with sparse vegetation. The east side of the mountain is a national forest.

There is a beautiful drive through the national forest on the east side. I have taken it many times. The juniper and ponderosa give way to the spruce trees that give way to the aspens. The environment changes at the end of the drive on the top of the mountain. The trees give way to rocks and sheer cliffs.

However, abundance exists on the west side of the mountain too!

The top part of the west side of the mountain has funny looking trees.

They lean towards the east. The prevailing winds are so consistent and strong that the trees are not able to grow straight. The winds push them at an angle. These trees grow out of solid rock in the midst of consistent wind.

These trees face tremendous obstacles in this harsh environment. The wind batters them. The sun bakes them. The rain avoids them. Still, they manage to live. The Law of Abundance mandates that they thrive.

Of course, if you look closely around these larger trees, you will observe other, baby trees, making their way out of the rocks. They serve as an example of how nature reproduces through multiplication.

Sheri and I observe this in our lives also. Nineteen months after the twins' birth, we add a baby girl to our family, and then, every other year for the next ten years, we add another child. The Law of Abundance allows us to reproduce through multiplication.

Examples of the Law of Abundance are everywhere. If you live in an urban environment, thank the Law of Abundance the next time you wait in line at the grocery or you become stuck in a traffic jam. The Law of Abundance is a universal principle.

Drive around in the poorest neighborhoods and look at the abundance. Notice the collection of possessions. The possessions may not be your choice of possessions but they are abundant. They could be broken down cars, dogs on a porch, or a plethora of plastic pink flamingos. Whatever you see, I promise you it will be a demonstration of abundance.

Look around where you live. Do you have enough room to store everything you have? Are closets and garages jammed full of abundance? Do you have enough time in the day to do what you want to do? Is your day crammed with an abundance of activities?

As you can see, abundance naturally happens everywhere.

Of course, that leaves the question. If the Law of Abundance is true, then why do we sometimes observe lack or feel like we don't have enough?

Financial Peace of Mind

Conspiracy Question

What evidence of reproduction through multiplication do I see?

Chapter 53

Robert faces that question after he returns from Vietnam in 1971. He finishes his enlistment period and comes home to Santa Fe.

The residual mental and emotional trauma of the war gnaws at him.

He works as a private pilot for wealthy business owners. He helps with his dad's real estate business. He occupies himself with a multitude of tasks. However, he does not experience peace.

After almost 20 years of this internal conflict, Robert decides to take an audacious step to find peace.

In 1989, he joins a group of Vietnam Veterans in planning a trip to go back and see the country where they lived and fought. Robert hopes he can experience resolution.

Interestingly enough, the government doesn't want them to go to Vietnam. It is illegal to fly from the United States to Vietnam. There is lack. However, airplane flights are abundant. They plan a flight from the United States to Canada to Vietnam.

The government responds by freezing their domestic bank accounts. They experience more lack.

However, money is abundant.

The men anticipate this action and already have funds in overseas accounts.

These men are soldiers and they know how to accomplish their mission.

As the day for departure draws near, the local New Mexico media focuses attention on Robert's trip.

Robert doesn't like the attention because it distracts from his travel plans. As a result, he almost doesn't respond when he receives a request from a station where he has already fulfilled one interview request.

He is resistant.

However, he senses this request is different.

It is.

A young man had contacted the station and requested that he be able to talk with Robert before the trip to Vietnam. It isn't convenient. However, they squeeze in a meeting the day before departure.

As a ten-year-old boy, this young man was one of the last people to board one of the last boats that left Vietnam before the Communists took command. He ended up in Santa Fe, adopted by an American family.

Now, as a young man, he has an envelope addressed to the rest of the family. It has Vietnamese postage and a request. Could Robert place the envelope into the Vietnam mail system for delivery to his family?

Robert knows he cannot do this.

He knows that entry to Vietnam includes a thorough search of his luggage. If the search revels anything beyond personal effects, he will lose those items and be turned away at the border.

Again, Robert experiences more lack and resistance. Again, Robert responds with abundance.

He takes the envelope and agrees to deliver it to the Vietnamese postage system.

When he arrives home from the meeting, he carefully removes the lining of his suitcase, places the envelope under the lining, and sews it back into place.

His experiences clearly demonstrate the next element in the Law of Abundance.

Conspiracy Question

What outside circumstances prevent my abundance?

Chapter 54

ELEMENT TWO: Lack is Always Temporary

Once I learn that abundance always happens. I have to ask the question, "Why do I sometimes see lack?"

For example, a fire wipes out a forest leaving a barren wasteland that appears void of life. The same fire escapes the forest and moves into a residential area destroying homes and possessions. The owners of those items experience lack.

Or, in another example, a hurricane produces a flood that devastates a coastal environment. The flood overruns levees and other barriers. It destroys residential and commercial structures. The owners of these properties experience lack.

As I think about it, I realize that, in each case, the lack is temporary. The remnants of the fire produce an environment that allows life to rejuvenate quickly. The flood scrubs and cleans the coastal area of pollutants so that life can thrive in an unprecedented manner.

The property owners in these areas rebuild completely or move to a different area where they may experience abundance.

These natural "disaster" examples demonstrate the Law of Abundance at work to create increased resources through first creating temporary lack. They teach a valuable lesson.

They teach the lesson that the only cause of lack is preparation for abundance.

Preparation for abundance is normal. Let's look closer.

The elements of nature, (wind, water, earth, and fire) function through movement. If something blocks that movement, lack occurs.

A dammed river produces a lake above the dam. Downstream, areas that once benefitted from the water now turn brown.

However, the movement continues. The blockage cannot remain in place forever. It must eventually yield to the movement or break.

A dam must release water periodically or it will break.

The buildup and release of pressure occurs throughout nature and throughout life.

The size of the buildup determines the violence of the release. Nature removes brush buildup with fire.

For years, the United States National Park Service saw fire as an enemy. When a fire started, they put it out immediately. After doing this for decades, they realized that some of the fires were so large they couldn't control them.

The reason is that fire is part of the flow of nature. If man doesn't interfere, the forests self-maintain themselves and a fire burns for hours or days. If man interferes, the resulting fires are so big they burn for weeks or months. The forests maintain themselves either way. They can do so gently or with great violence.

The amount of brush determines the violence of the fire.

Other natural examples of buildup and release include earthquakes and weather storms.

When a buildup happens in a person's body, the results include heart attacks, constipation, strokes, and acne. Sometimes great force such as surgery and other invasive treatments must release the blockage. Meanwhile, exercise, peaceful thinking, and proper diet keep the body's systems flowing and prevent these symptoms.

Violent releases often produce dramatic results. In nature, violent releases produced some of the United States National Parks including Grand Canyon, Zion Canyon, Yellowstone, and Yosemite.

The lesson I learn is that The Law of Abundance always works.

When The Law of Abundance flows, life is gentle. When The Law of Abundance is blocked, there is temporary lack until release happens in a dramatic and often violent breakthrough.

I decide I want a gentle life, a life of peace and happiness.

In my search for peace, I realize that unity brings love and love brings peace.

I realize that lack is a perspective of duality.

When I have a perspective of unity, the destructive fire that causes lack is an abundance of fire. The raging storm that destroys property is an abundance of wind and water.

Abundance always produces abundance. There is no such thing as permanent lack.

When I have a perspective of duality, I see lack.

My perspective of lack is a warning. It is a red flag.

Lack is an indicator that my perspective has shifted from unity to duality.

Once I realize this, I discover there are other red flags that indicate I am looking at something from the perspective of duality instead of my Desired perspective of unity.

In the section *Relationship Peace of Mind, How to Live Within the Law of Attraction*, I demonstrate that the only way to have relationship peace is through a change in perspective. Most of us have a perspective of duality because we live in an illusionary world of duality that operates over a reality of unity.

However, the secret to peace is a perspective of unity. It is a perspective that says, no matter what happens, it is part of a greater good that produces the best for me.

It is a Conspiracy for Me!

Conspiracy Question

What does "Conspiracy for Me" mean to me?

Chapter 55

I believe that everything that happens in life is part of a Conspiracy for Me.

This cornerstone of the Living the Southwest Lifestyle philosophy means that I choose to live from a perspective of unity rather than a perspective of duality.

This perspective allows me to love all. It allows me to pursue my Desire. It allows me to experience the free flow of miracles into my life.

However, because our society usually sees things through a perspective of duality, I find it easy and natural to move back to a perspective of duality.

Elections, religions, sports, and business appear to consist of "us versus them."

The world appears to operate based on hot/cold, white/black, rich/poor, and right/wrong.

A perspective of duality is easy to believe. It causes guilt, blame, and fear.

I once believed in duality so much that I thought conflict and resolution were the basis of life. Superficial observation confirmed this to me so I thought duality was the truth.

In addition, duality is the basis of drama. The emotion that goes with drama creates adrenaline and produces a physical high.

I was so addicted to the high caused by drama that if my life did not contain drama, I created it.

I lived a life based on guilt, blame, and fear. If I was not experiencing the high from guilt, blame, and fear, I created situations that brought those things to me.

Once I become convinced that changing perspective from duality to unity is a worthy goal, I discover obstacles to the change. All of these obstacles are thoughts I have learned over my life. They are techniques I learned to survive in a world of duality.

These obstacles are easy to overcome when I recognize them. My Desire to love others allows me to experience The Law of Miracles. I break old habits and form new ones in a matter of days or hours rather in three to four weeks.

However, some of these obstacles are subtle.
Guilt feels like humility and gives me an excuse not to love myself so I can better love others.

Blame allows me to love myself because other people do the same thing so I think I'm not so bad.

Fear feels like love because I'm protecting myself and others from outside dangers.

Guilt, blame, and fear disguise themselves as love so I have trouble recognizing them.

Therefore, I need clues to see guilt, blame, and fear. I call those clues "red flags" because they are warnings that something needs attention. They tell me that I'm looking at something from the perspective of duality.

They tell me that the love I think I am feeling is really guilt, blame, or fear.

Here is the list of red flags. Memorize it and you are on your way to a perspective of unity.

1. Resistance

That's it. Resistance

Whenever I'm resistant to anything that happens in my life, I'm out of the flow. I'm operating from a perspective of duality rather than a perspective of unity. I'm blocking my ability to recognize The Law of Abundance.

A red flag means guilt, blame, or fear exists. However, I don't feel guilt, blame, or fear. I feel love combined with resistance.

Every time I feel resistance, there is underlying guilt, blame, or fear causing that resistance.

Resistance is THE red flag.

> **Conspiracy Question**
>
> What causes me to feel resistance?
>
> Is it my crazy ideas?
>
> Do I have hang-ups over money?
>
> Am I struggling with how I'm going to pay bills?
>
> Am I upset because the government is spending too much money?

Chapter 56

Let's look closer at resistance.

War is the ultimate external demonstration of internal resistance and part of Robert's purpose in going to Vietnam again is to release the emotions of the conflict he participated in twenty years earlier.

He doesn't consciously know that. However, the Conspiracy for Him knows that and it compels him to take the trip, smuggle the envelope, and then, forget about it.

The trip is everything Robert and his co-travelers had hoped. No one notices the envelope in the suitcase and Robert almost brings it back to the United States with him.

He only has one day left in his trip when he remembers to remove it from the lining of his suitcase.

If Robert had remembered earlier, he would have just dropped the envelope into the mail.

However, on this day, he looks at the envelope and realizes that, for the first time on the trip, he is in the same city that is in the address on the envelope.

He can't just drop it in a mailbox. He has to deliver the envelope personally.

Can you imagine the emotions the family feels as an American comes to their door? They are afraid, uncertain, and tentative. They do not understand this white man and he doesn't understand them.

Then, Robert pulls out the envelope and begins to share the pictures. The confusion turns to joy and elation. It is as if a lost family member had been raised from the dead.

By the time the evening is complete, Robert has pictures, letters, and hugs to smuggle out of the country.

In addition, he had a faint hope of bringing the family together in the United States.

Robert knows this is impossible. There is no legal way for citizens of Vietnam to leave the country.

He also knows he may have put the family members' lives in danger by visiting.

At one time, this family held a prominent place in Saigon. The father owned an automotive dealership. However, as the events of the early 1970s happen, he takes steps to move his family out of Vietnam.

He gives his oldest son money to pay bribes. The son succeeds in leaving. The youngest son gets on a refuge boat.

However, neither son can succeed in helping the rest of the family escape. The Communist takeover happens too quickly.

Authorities execute the prominent father, leaving behind six women covering three generations.

Now, Robert has given life to a hope that appears impossible to fulfill.

Conspiracy Question

What am I resistant to in my life today?

Chapter 57

I love the Adidas commercials that say, "Impossible is nothing." I firmly believe that impossible is just an opinion.

The opinion that something is impossible is nothing more than resistance.

Resisting anything in my life is like driving a sports car as fast as I can with my foot on the brake. It is violent, loud, and unproductive.

When something arrives into my life, it is too late to change it. It is too late to do anything about it. I can only accept it and respond. I cannot change it.

When I complain and resist, I become like that sports car. I am violent, loud, and unproductive. Resistance creates drama.

If I believe in The Law of Attraction, I attract everything into my life. If I attract a challenge into my life, I attracted it to spotlight an area of resistance that I need to remove. It really is that simple.

If I feel like hiding, I'm resisting what I have attracted into my life. I feel guilty

If I feel hurt, I'm resisting the good that I can receive from the situation. I am blaming the situation.

If I see an opponent, I'm resisting the help that comes from his influence. I am blaming another person.

If I see lack, I'm resisting the truth of abundance. I'm afraid there isn't enough.

Resistance causes us to see lack where there is abundance. During our first year of marriage, Sheri and I have a perspective of duality. We see lack.

We think we will have a child during our first year of marriage. We do not.

Because we live within the dimension of time, Sheri and I use time to measure the speed of The Law of Abundance. While waiting to become pregnant with our first child, we think the process is taking too long.

This thought comes from a perspective of lack, a perspective of duality. This perspective says, "If you have something, I cannot have it." It is the basis of war and conflict.

We don't have one child after one year. For the first seven months of our marriage, until Sheri becomes pregnant, we experience what we think is lack.

However, we're in the perfect situation to learn about abundance. We have a large house to live in during the first 14 months of our marriage. It has six bedrooms and four bathrooms. It is an abundant house for newlyweds.

During that time, we offer a room to a local pregnancy center. One of their clients, a single, expectant mother, stays with us. Sheri learns about the pregnancy experience and is present when our houseguest gives birth.

In addition, a neighbor's cat decides to birth her kittens on our front porch. Sheri helps with the delivery.

These two experiences increase her understanding of pregnancy and delivery. This changes her perspective.

We begin to see abundance.

Then, Sheri becomes pregnant. We discover we're having twins, and we have two children after fourteen months instead of one child after twelve.

We experience a miracle, a shortcut in time and space. We experience abundance. This perspective says, "There is more than enough for everybody." It is the basis of peace.

Notice that our perspective of duality did not prevent The Law of Abundance from working. The law is always working. The perspective of duality only prevents recognition of The Law of Abundance.

With the perspective of duality, the new asphalt on our road slows down the growth of the plants underneath.

With the perspective of duality, a fire destroys trees.

With the perspective of duality, a flood wipes out a nesting area for wildlife.

With the perspective of duality, Sheri and I think we may never have children.

With the perspective of duality, five Vietnamese women panic when their family's house is broken into at 3 AM and strangers tell them they have ten minutes to pack. These women know execution is next because they spent time with Robert, the American.

With the perspective of unity, the plants benefit from the asphalt and grow through it.

With the perspective of unity, the fire creates the perfect environment for the seeds left behind to quickly germinate and create more trees.

With the perspective of unity, the flood leaves behind a clean area with greater capability for reproduction.

With the perspective of unity, Sheri and I realize that abundance is a normal act of nature and lack is always temporary.

With the perspective of unity, one Vietnamese woman remains calm when her family's house is broken into at 3 AM and strangers tell them they have ten minutes to pack. This woman knows it is a Conspiracy for Her.

Conspiracy Question

What impossible situation do I face today?

Chapter 58

The Law of Abundance is natural. It is life. It is always there. However, we often don't see it because of our perspective. We don't see it because we have blocked our view with resistance.

Resistance is sneaky. It is sometimes difficult to identify. I've learned some dramatic lessons about how the divine wants me to release it.

One took place in the winter of 2007. "How are you feeling Matthew?"

The voice is a friend from my past. It is someone I haven't seen in years, until today.

I giggle, and say "Hi Chuck."

I first meet Chuck in 1987. We work together for a couple of years doing telemarketing.

We each leave that job to start our own businesses. He and his wife need an accountant for their business. My business is accounting so they are my clients for several years.

When I cut back on my accounting practice to take a marketing position with a local gourmet food company, I release most of my clients including Chuck and his wife. It isn't personal. It is just business.

I slowly open my eyes and make eye contact with Chuck. He smiles an amused smile.

Am I dreaming?

I look at our dining room ceiling. Someone's finger is on my neck, taking my pulse.

I hear myself say, "I'm alive."

My wife, Sheri, says. "It's 50."

I smile and remember my resting pulse rate at age 18. It was 48. Now, at age 46, it is still slow and steady.

I am puzzled.

How did I get here – flat on the floor?

I'll answer that question in just a moment. First, let's look at the next element of The Law of Abundance.

ELEMENT THREE: Gratefulness accelerates The Law of Abundance.

This element is where all of the Laws of the Southwest Lifestyle come together.

Let's review.

The Law of Miracles works through understanding my Desire and using thoughts, words, actions, and habits to learn how to love.

Guilt, blame, and fear resist love and temporarily block the flow of miracles to me.

The Law of Attraction works with my emotional focus. When I am single-minded, the emotional intensity creates powerful waves that attract anything else vibrating at that frequency.

When I am confused, I emit two or more different frequencies. This prevents the intensity because the waves interfere with one another. My confusion temporarily blocks what I want to attract.

I cooperate with The Law of Miracles when I learn how to love. I cooperate with The Law of Attraction when I have a singular emotional focus.

I cooperate with The Law of Abundance when I express gratefulness.

The most powerful way to express gratefulness is through acts of generosity.

The emotion of gratefulness expressed through acts of generosity releases The Law of Abundance in my life.

Generosity removes all resistance.

Most of us have resistance in our lives, significant resistance. It shows up in our subconscious programming, in our defensive responses, and in our conflict.

If you picked up this book looking for financial secrets and money management tips, the material you read may disappoint you.

I do not apologize for this.

Everyone knows the basics of making and managing money.

I have a friend who has made a lot of money in his lifetime. He says that anyone can make money.

This begs the question. "If anyone can make money, why don't more people make money?"

The answer is simple. We know what to do. We resist doing it.

We don't realize that, to acquire new things, we must let go of old things. This letting go process is necessary for abundance.

Most of us would rather live in the security of our poverty than experience the uncertainty of the potential of abundance.

We are afraid we will lose the things we have if we let go of them. We are afraid of what might happen if we let go of what we have so we miss pure potential.

We do this with people too. We look for one person to fulfill us or complete us and we resist all others. We are afraid of what might happen if we let go of what we have so we miss pure potential.

This letting go process is necessary for abundance. However, as I said before, most of us would rather live in the security of our poverty than experience the uncertainty of the potential of abundance.

I could use this book to tell you about the importance of:

- Networking
- The law of harvest
- Spending to earnings ratio

- Marketing
- Sales conversions
- Creating value and selling higher priced products

However, if you are resistant to these ideas, this will not help you. In addition, I could use this book tell you to:

- Give money away
- Get clear
- Take the most likely action
- Support a cause
- Get support
- Be grateful
- Do what you love
- Expect success

However, if you are resistant because you have limiting beliefs about money, this will not help you.

For example, if you believe:

- "Money is evil."
- "Money will attract problems."
- "Money will make me a selfish person."
- "Wanting money is greedy."
- "Rich people are snobs."

The financial information listed above will not help you.

If you have a financial thermostat that is not comfortable with significant amounts of money, the financial information listed above will not help you.

I know what it takes to help other people achieve abundance.

I've spent countless hours coaching thousands of people on how to make money.

Everyone I coach agrees with my ideas. In fact, I could talk to you for several hours about how to make money and you would agree with my ideas too.

Making money is easy.

However, people who don't have enough money and don't have financial peace of mind always have a great deal of resistance in their lives.

In fact, resistance is so ingrained in our society that we will cling to it in the face of great suffering.

I'll say it again.

Most of us would rather live in the security of our poverty than experience the uncertainty of the potential of abundance.

My observation is that if a person understands how to release resistance, he or she can experience abundance.

However, most people are so resistant that no amount of financial instructions can help.

Therefore, the next several chapters demonstrate how the Conspiracy for Me worked in my life and the lives of my friends and family to help release resistance.

Once you understand the significance of releasing resistance, then I suggest you contact Peace of Mind Training Institute offices and schedule coaching to assist you in acquiring abundance and wealth. (See the back of this book for contact information.)

Conspiracy Question

What thoughts do I have that resist abundance?

Chapter 59

Earlier, I wrote about waking up on our dining room floor. I think, "How did I get here?"

I hit the rewind button on my brain in an attempt to remember. I go back an hour.

I finish the weekly afternoon basketball games, shower, and start to help Sheri host our annual Holiday Open House.

It is good to see our guests. The fascinating conversations flow freely over food and drink.

I excuse myself from one conversation to step towards the restroom and then…

Well, I'm not sure what happens.

I remember hearing someone bump into our dining room table. Was that someone me?

I remember Sheri saying, "What's going on here?" I must have passed out.

Yes, I was feeling a little dizzy. I remember thinking, "I should eat something."

Now, I'm flat on the floor, looking up at our guests while my wife goes from taking my pulse to taking my blood pressure.

Someone asks, "Does he have low blood pressure?"

I have no idea. I stay away from doctors because I feel great. Sheri responds by saying, "84 over 46."

I get up off the floor. I'm still a little dizzy. I lay down on a row of our dining room chairs. Someone brings me an orange to eat.

A few minutes later, Sheri takes my pulse and blood pressure again. The numbers are normal. My pulse is 74 and my blood pressure is 108 over 68.

I know enough about diet, sugar levels, and protein to know what happened physically. I exerted myself (by playing basketball); I didn't eat property (I didn't eat anything. I only had a small glass of wine.), and I passed out. I'm not the first person to do this. However, this is my first time doing it.

Within thirty minutes, I'm on my feet, chatting with guests, and continuing the evening as if nothing has happened.

However, something has changed.

My brain re-wired during that trip to the floor. I hear it in my conversation. I feel it in my thinking. I sense it in my emotions.

I slipped "through the looking glass." I went down the rabbit hole and over to the other side.

I now know it was simply an act of releasing resistance.

We all do it. Sometimes, this experience is easy and relaxed. On rare occasions, it includes the phenomenon of "passing out" while having a spiritual experience.

Even rarer, someone enters a coma and comes out a different person.

Why are the experiences different? Do we have a spiritual encounter every time we "pass out," including sleep? Can we consciously use our unconscious time to deepen our spiritual understanding?

I have found the answers to these questions and I am certain you will experience increased understanding as you read this book.

In the following chapters, you will read several dramatic personal stories about releasing resistance, including my first public encounter with this experience in the early 1980s and my subsequent research on the topic.

I will tell you about a young man who experienced a personality change because of his journey to the other side. I'm glad he took the journey because his wife is my daughter, Mary. His new personality and temperament fit perfectly into our family.

We will explore how resistance affected my health, the health of my children, and the health of my clients.

You will read the story of how one of my clients became a stranger to his family when he dramatically learned how to love.

In addition, this book's bonus material includes a list of common questions and answers on this phenomenon.
As you read these stories, I ask you to look for this pattern:

1. The Law of Attraction says I attract everything into my life.
2. If that is true, when I resist what arrives, it means I'm opposing the very thing I attracted.
3. This resistance creates an internal conflict.
4. I may recognize this conflict and release it through a religious experience or dream.
5. If I choose not to release the resistance, I may pass out, faint, become sick, or even end up in a coma in order for the resistance to disappear.

These stories dramatically demonstrate that releasing resistance is vital to your well-being.

> **Conspiracy Question**
>
> Have I ever passed out? What happened?
>
> Describe it.
>
> What did I learn?

Chapter 60

The heat and humidity of Eastern North Carolina chase me into the old storefront that serves as the meeting place for the new church in town.

I am a recent graduate of East Carolina University with a degree in Music Education. I like the community and I like my current job so I decide to remain in the area after graduation.

The job is outside my field of study. However, it puts money in my pocket and I like my boss. He is a spiritual man who encourages my spiritual searching. On this evening, I'm taking his advice and going to a church I've only heard about from him.

This isn't their regular church service. They are participating in a satellite simulcast with churches throughout the country. It originates from a "mega-church" in Texas. They show the live Texas church service through a satellite feed projected on a screen that hangs from the ceiling.

Because of the difference in time zones, it begins an hour later than usual. I start the evening by attending my regular Sunday evening church service and arrive here just as the lights go down and the simulcast starts.

The message I hear is new and fresh to me. It still resonates within me today. However, the evening will be memorable for other reasons too.

Once the preaching in Texas is complete, the local pastor grabs the microphone, and asks someone to turn off the projector and raise the screen.

He says, "The Spirit of the Lord is in this place and He is going to do something special tonight. Lift your hands and praise the Lord."

I'm sitting halfway back in the long thin room. I look around me. I'm not sure what to do. I've attended church all my life but this is new to me. I'm familiar with hymns, reverence and quiet praise – with my eyes closed. I only raise my hand if I have a question.

The crowd stands so I stand. I do what they do. They raise their hands. I raise my hands. I don't close my eyes.

I want to see what will happen next.

I wonder if the pastor really senses something supernatural or if he is just a charismatic leader preparing to manipulate the people into a frenzy.

After a few minutes, he lets out a yell and says, "WOO! I can feel the power of God in my hands. If you want God's Spirit to heal your sickness, relieve your depression, and meet whatever need you have, come up here, and I'll pray for you and lay hands on you."

I think I understand what is going on now. It is an "altar call." I've seen them in every church I've attended. People touched by the message now have an opportunity to be saved, join the church, or receive prayer. I've seen them many times. I relax at the familiarity.

I don't stay relaxed for long.

The pastor approaches the first person, a woman, and prays for her. He touches her head and, much to my surprise, she falls backward.

Is she dead? Did she faint?

I look around me to see if anyone else is surprised. People are smiling. No one jumps or seems alarmed.

Maybe that's normal at this church. However, it isn't normal to me. What is going on here?

People now rush to be prayed for. Other people want to receive this "blessing." This appears to be something special.

The pastor prays for the next person, a man. He touches him on the head and he falls backward too.

Now, it seems that everyone is moving at once. Some leave the building. Most move forward. I'm not sure I want to be prayed for but I want a better look at what is happening so I move forward too.

From my new vantage point, I see everything now. The pastor prays for the next person, another woman. She falls backward too. Two men catch her and help her to the floor. A young woman quickly places a sheet over her lower legs. (I learn later that the sheet is for "modesty.")

I look around me. There is a mixture of people - young, old, black, white, men, and women - in the building.

The prayer line is long and the pastor continues to pray and touch each person on the forehead. Most people fall. Some do not.

He asks people to come forward and pray for him as he ministers. It is a good excuse for me to get even closer to the action. I move towards a group of people who are praying with their eyes open and their arms outstretched.

I join them. I have to know what is going on. I pretend to pray while I look on in wide-eyed amazement.

As I watch, I think back to previous conversations with spiritual leaders about supernatural happenings. Some say that everything supernatural is evil. Others say it happened for Jesus and the disciples but not for us today. Still others say that supernatural manifestations are real and that they happen today.

My heart tells me miracles could happen today. However, I've never seen one so I don't have proof.

Now, as I stand watching the prayer line in front of me, I think I might have proof – unless it is all an act or the scene playing out in front of me is an elaborate stage production.

I start to look at the events critically.

Maybe the pastor is pushing them down. He doesn't seem to be.

Maybe everyone is falling down because that is what everyone expects.

I am not sure. I look closer. I can't tell.

I wonder how long this will continue. People get up from the floor. Some walk to the back of the building and leave. Others join our group to pray for the pastor as he ministers. I watch one woman as she goes to the back of the prayer line to go through again.

I think to myself. "Did she not get enough the first time? Does she have an insatiable need for attention?"

I lose track of time. I'm caught between wanting to believe this is a real move of God and trying to figure out if the entire thing is fake.

The pastor stops praying for people and picks up the microphone. He looks ashen.

"The physical body cannot always handle the energy that comes from carrying the Spirit of the Lord. I am tired. I feel the anointing in my hands and I know there are needs but I don't know how long I can physically continue to minister tonight."

If this is a staged drama, the plot has just taken a new twist. He continues.

"Will someone come help me? I want someone to come, receive the anointing from my hands, and keep praying for the people."

It is like a scene from the Old Testament story of Moses holding up his arms over the battlefield. When Moses lifts up his arms, the children of Israel prevail in the battle. When his arms tire and he lowers them, the enemy prevails. The only way Israel wins the battle is for two people to hold up Moses' tired arms.

This pastor needs someone to hold up his arms.

A young black man approaches the stage. He volunteers to help.

The pastor looks relieved. He puts down the microphone and steps to the left side of the platform with the young man.

The moment seems significant. I watch it closely. Another Biblical story comes to mind. This time it is the prophet Elijah passing his mantle to Elisha.

The pastor leans against the wall, almost unable to continue. He tells the young man to face him and raise his hands.

As the young man raises his hands and closes his eyes, the pastor raises his hands and touches the younger man's hands. As soon as they touch, the younger man flies backward across the stage. The pastor collapses against the wall and crumbles to the floor.

I can question and reason away everything I witness this evening. However, I cannot find a reasonable explanation for what I just saw. Some unseen energy propelled the young man across the stage.

This single event validates the entire evening.

Several people help the pastor to his feet and lead him to a chair. The younger man moves to the prayer line, ministering to the people.

The evening continues as a blur. At some point, I leave to go home. The clock in my car says it is after midnight. I have been at church more than four hours.

That event, in the summer of 1983, was the first time I witnessed physical bodies collapsing under the power of something supernatural.

It wasn't the last.

Since that time, I have observed, experienced, and read about this phenomenon. It is both fascinating and surreal.

Each time I experience it, I feel elated and intrigued. I have to know more and experience it again. However, it takes more than 25 years for me to understand it.

One story that is the key to my understanding is the near death experience of my son-in-law. It begins in the next chapter

> **Conspiracy Question**
>
> Have I seen other people pass out? What happened?
>
> Describe it.
>
> What did I learn?

Chapter 61

"Let's take one more run down the mountain."

I agree and we head for the lifts with snowboards in hand.

The first Saturday of March in 2005 is a clear and sunny day. The snow at Santa Fe Ski Area is a mix of powder and slush as I refine my beginning snowboarding skills with numerous runs down the mountain.

Now, as the sun heads towards the horizon and the temperature drops, we ride the lift to the top for one more run. We will finish this run, call it a day, and drive home to an evening of dinner and video games.

We unload from the lift. My friend quickly straps on his board and goes ahead. I'm a little slower. I want to take in the beautiful New Mexico scenery laid out before me one more time before I start my run.

With my sightseeing complete, I head down the mountain.

I've fallen a few times today without injury. Falling isn't so bad if you know how to do it and I know how because I play football. On this trip, I fall once, then again, breaking my fall by landing softly in the slushy snow.

The next part of my trip takes me down the mountain and into a shady spot to make a right hand turn. My toe edge catches a newly formed patch of ice. The ice serves as a ramp for my board, throwing me backwards. I fall, hitting my head on the ice.

I don't remember landing.

I don't remember the paramedics cutting the ski coat off my still body.

I don't remember the helicopter ride from 11,000 elevation down to Saint Vincent hospital in Santa Fe.

I am not there when the doctors gather my parents and friends in the counseling area to tell them I will not live through the night.

I don't remember the next day when two friends hold my hands and ask me to squeeze if I can hear them. I squeeze. They have hope. I don't remember.

I don't remember anything that happens between that beautiful Saturday afternoon and three days later when I wake up with a pounding headache.

However, within two weeks of my fall, after numerous tests, surgery to remove fluid on my brain, and a recovery period, I check out of the hospital.

I am a different person. Prior to the accident, I remember being selfish. I remember being the only one that matters. I remember not listening to counsel.

My friends tell me I was angry. They laugh about the time I destroyed a parking lot reflector post because I had to go to work. They tell me how I would explode if someone made fun of me.

Those memories are a distant past to me. When I hear the stories now, it feels like they are talking about someone else.

I am a different person. I'm more open-minded. I am less resistant. I am kinder, softer, less controlling.

Something happened during those three days to change my personality from harsh to kind, angry to meek, closed to opened.

It was as if I was traveling down the freeway of life, selfishly going my own way, and took a freeway exit to avoid some unknown self-destruction ahead.

Jon's story dramatically demonstrates how he released emotional resistance. However, sometimes the resistance is physical and requires medical assistance.

Those stories begin in the next chapter.

> **Conspiracy Question**
>
> Have you experienced a life threatening accident?
>
> Write it out and identify the lessons you learned from it.

Chapter 62

My wife and I have eight children. Since we started with twins and had another child nineteen months later, we quickly became accustomed to diapers and potty training.

More than once, there was an "accident" that meant washing the bed sheets. However, as the children grew older, each learned to control his or her nighttime need to use the restroom. The accidents became less frequent with everyone except our fourth child, Paul.

In addition to an occasional wet bed, Paul's early morning routine includes nausea. He is also the only one of our children to experience motion sickness. The problems worsen after his eleventh birthday and we seek medical help.

Our family doctor can't diagnose the problem so she refers Paul to a specialist. After a round of tests, the doctor finds the source of the problem and decides to perform a medulla decompression.

This is surgical procedure where the doctors make a three-inch incision in the back of the skull and use a dental drill to shave away bone.

The simple explanation is Paul's brain is too big for his skull. This isn't a significant problem during the day.

However, at night, when Paul is sleeping, spinal fluid flows from the brain into the spine. If the path between the two is open, everything is fine and normal. When there is resistance on that path, as in Paul's case, pressure builds in the brain. This pressure stimulates the brain to release the bladder and produces nausea.

The procedure is successful and Paul's problems leave immediately - as soon as the doctors carve away the resistance.

Paul's surgery reminds me that, as a child, I have similar issues. Bed-wetting isn't an issue for me. My problem is nausea.

As a child, I am always "car sick." It is so bad that I get sick on a 15-minute trip across town.

In the summer of 1978, I am sixteen years old and the carsickness still lingers. I wonder how my tummy will do over the next few weeks. I have just finished a week of rehearsal with the All-Student Marching Band USA and we're heading to Dulles Airport just outside Washington DC for our overnight flight to London.

We'll tour Europe for three weeks.

Our flight leaves at 9 PM. It is the Fourth of July and, as we fly over DC and Baltimore, I see the fireworks coming up towards our plane.

I don't sleep much during the flight and, as we prepare to land, I discover that carsickness and "air sickness" are the same thing. I wonder how many days I'll be sick on this tour.

We land in London at 9 in the morning, go through customs, and board a bus to Cardiff Wales. We have a 4 PM formal reception.

We ride the bus for six hours. I won't eat so I can be nausea free for the entire ride. We attend the reception, enjoy a nice meal, and board the bus back to the University of Wales where we will spend the night.

I fall asleep on the ride across town. When I awake, a friend is gently shaking me and the tour nurse is boarding the bus with a concerned look.

I get up to leave. The nurse asks, "Are you OK?" I'm puzzled. "Yes, I'm fine. Why shouldn't I be?" My friend quickly explains.

"Everyone got off the bus but you were asleep. I tried to wake you up but you wouldn't budge. I panicked and slapped you. Man, I slapped you hard and you wouldn't wake up so I asked someone to send the nurse."

I shrug. I feel fine.

In fact, I feel great through the rest of the trip. We tour Wales and London. I experience amusement park rides for the first time without nausea.

We take an overnight ferry from Dover to France. We tour the European mainland including the Alps. We travel along narrow switchback roads with curves so tight that the buses have to back up to get through them. I never experience carsickness again.

Although I never had tests run, the circumstantial evidence is that I had a condition similar to Paul's but less severe. I released my carsickness during the trip across Cardiff. Paul released his through the surgical procedure.

My daughter, Mary, experiences release in another manner. She passes out while driving a loaded van.

> **Conspiracy Question**
>
> How do I release sickness?
>
> Do I use traditional western medicine (surgery or medication) or another method?
>
> Write about it.

Chapter 63

"Oh no, he's slowing down too fast!"

I slam on the breaks to avoid hitting the vehicle in front of me. The pile of gift boxes stacked in the van collides with the back of my head. I black out.

It is a rainy Thursday evening and we're moving stuff from the old warehouse to the new one. I knew we had packed the flat, empty boxes too high when we put them in the van. Rather than repack them, I decided I would be careful driving home.

However, I didn't account for the unexpected and now, I'm passed out behind the wheel of a loaded van on a public road.

I feel something scratch my face. My sister, Deborah, is moving the boxes back into place. She unintentionally skims my face with the gift boxes.

I evaluate what happened. I look around. Everything is blurry. The brake lights in front of me tell me that we didn't get in an accident. It is still raining. The light is still red. I was only out for a brief moment.

Deborah asks if I'm okay. My head is throbbing but it doesn't hurt. The skin on my neck is numb but it doesn't hurt. *If nothing hurts, then why am I crying?*

I return home. I'm thirty-six weeks pregnant so I let everyone else unload the van. I sit down and relax until dinnertime. I continue a book I borrowed from my midwife. I don't realize it contains the answer to my question.

I start chapter nine, "Easing pain in labor – what you can do?"

Before I read, I think back to earlier experiences with pain. My childhood contained an assortment of arm and leg injuries. Once an injury happened, the pain always seemed to be there, even years afterwards. In fact, my simple arm injury required surgery and the pain never went away – until recently.

I subconsciously know that childbirth will be more painful. In fact, I have already felt more pain through the occasional contraction than I felt with that arm injury. My perspective has changed.

It is about to change again.

A sentence leaps off the page at me. "Childbirth doesn't have to be painful!" I haven't thought much of giving birth in the last few months. I convinced myself that worrying about it was only going to make it worse. Regardless of other people's horror stories, I've decided that my birth experience is going to be a positive one.

I continue reading and discover that pain has a purpose. It serves notice that we need to make a change. It is usually the result of fear or tension or a combination of the two.

So it is with pain during labor. It is a signal that implies the woman needs to relax. When a woman is relaxed, the sensations of her contractions signal that labor is progressing normally and she can simply let it happen.

However, because women have been conditioned to expect pain in childbirth, they often discount its significance as a signal. Instead, they tense up in anticipation of the pain. They become afraid of the pain being more than they can handle.

The so-called "fear-tension-pain cycle" takes over.

It hits me! That is why I cried in the van. I expected pain so I tensed. I was afraid of pain so I looked for it. However, there was no pain.

I blacked out because of fear. The lightweight gift boxes weighed too little and traveled too short a distance to hurt me. Had the injury been serious, I wouldn't have "come to" so quickly.

There was no injury at all. My neck was not scraped or bruised. The pain I thought I felt was the fear of something dreadful. I passed out and "came to" immediately because once I had passed out, I "knew" I wasn't hurt.

I made a change in perspective.

I decide childbirth will be the same for me. When I feel pain, I will make changes that alleviate the pain. I will not be afraid of the pain. I will not tense up. I will relax and enjoy the experience.

Unmanageable pain during birth is not normal! Even in athletic training, the old axiom "no pain-no gain" has been disproven. When a muscle hurts, its function is compromised, and it is more prone to injury.

In labor, the less the pain, the more the gain. Pain in labor stimulates release of hormones that inhibit labor. I do not have to hurt to deliver a baby. Pain, properly understood and sensitively managed, is a valuable labor assistant. I will listen to its signals and adjust.

The most dramatic story of release comes from one of my clients. Turn the page to read it.

> **Conspiracy Question**
>
> What pain and or sickness do I currently experience?
>
> Do I use pain to prevent abundance? How do I do this?

Chapter 64

The cool air hits Frank's face as he enters the garage.

December means cooler temperatures. It also means Christmas will be here soon so Frank begins his annual trip to the attic in search of holiday decorations.

He pulls down the attic entrance and sets the stairs in place on the garage floor. He is not sure what happens next.

Later that day, his daughter discovers Frank unconscious on the garage floor. Years later, Frank still has no idea how he got there.

Did the attic stairs shift? Did he trip? Did he hit his head on the attic entrance?

Frank feels fine when he regains consciousness. However, the next few months are a mix of clarity and blurry visions.

Frank's brain rewires. He loses short-term memory and gains memories from his young childhood – memories he had lost.

Frank's personality shifts. He loses his tact and sense of humor. He gains love for strangers and the homeless.

Frank goes through medical tests. The medical experts who review tests find nothing to indicate the cause of his changes.

He begins to experience extraordinary mood swings of euphoria followed by depression.

He continues to work as a counselor. Five months later, he receives the best evaluations he has ever received on his job.

Frank loses the ability to sleep for more than an hour at a time. He gains a connection with spirituality that occasionally enables him to perceive another dimension.

His changes are so dramatic that his wife starts a journal entitled *A Stranger in the House*.

Months later, a relative notices an abnormality on Frank's CAT scan that other medical professionals have missed.
The medical evidence shows that Frank has a brain injury.

He receives treatment and medication that relieves some of the symptoms. However, the source of the healing is deeper than a pill or counselor can reach.

It comes from his heart, through an unexpected source.

Frank's daughter, the same daughter who found him on the floor in the garage on that cold December day, enters a crucial time in her life.

She marries an abusive husband. Frank's emotions stabilize. Instead of swinging from euphoria to depression, they become only worry and anger.

From his professional training, Frank knows the symptoms and patterns of an abusive husband. He worries that his daughter may be murdered.

He is angry that someone, anyone would consider hurting his daughter.

One morning, as he sits in his home, God asks Frank, "Who do you love more, me or your daughter?"

He knows God is asking the question to him. He doesn't doubt the inner voice or the source of the question.

Frank wrestles with the answer. Finally, he apologizes to God and says, "I'm sorry. However, I love my daughter more."

The next morning God speaks again. "Frank, I love your daughter more than you can ever love her. I love you more than you can imagine. Surrender to me and trust me. I won't let you down."

Frank considers releasing the emotions and trusting God. He attends church the next Sunday morning and the pastor introduces the story of Abraham and Isaac. God asks Abraham the question, "Who do you love more, me or your son?"

Frank has confirmation that God spoke to him that week. He releases his daughter to God.

In just a few days, his son-in-law locks his daughter in the bathroom of their home. It would be a potential SWAT situation except that she cannot contact anyone for help.

Instead, she has anticipated this possibility and has her own plan. She escapes and flees to a relative's home.

From there, she finally decides to do what other people have suggested. She files a restraining order against her husband.

The authorities serve the restraining order. Her husband responds by committing suicide.

The husband's family blames her for his death. She is not allowed to attend the Memorial Service.

In response, Frank arranges a private service for his daughter. She is able to experience closure to the relationship with her late husband.

The drama concludes.

Looking back, it is obvious that healing has taken place. However, this healing isn't about avoiding death, overcoming grief, or recovering from a brain injury.

Instead, it is about learning to love.

Frank's daughter in this story is his adopted daughter. Prior to Franks accident, he loved and cared for her. However, something was missing.

Subconsciously, Frank wanted to learn to love all at all times. However, he didn't know how to do that.

Through his accident, he learned to love all. He started talking to strangers. He developed an interest in homeless people.

In addition, he developed counseling skills that were recognized by his peers and clients.

However, the side effects of his accident pushed him out of balance. The medical treatment helped but it wasn't enough.

It took his daughter's drama to bring him back.

Suddenly his physical condition wasn't the most important thing in his life. When he focused his emotional energy on his daughter, something shifted in him.

He learned to release.

He released his daughter to God. He released his resistance to love.

> **Conspiracy Question**
>
> How do I resist Love?

Chapter 65

During the time I was recording these stories, one of my clients told me a story about her daughter, Christine (not her real name).

She had no knowledge of my topic and she only told the story in response to my asking, "How is your daughter?"

Christine is currently four years old.

Our client says that, for the past two years, about a week before her daughter's birthdays and half birthdays, her daughter becomes sick.

Then, she experiences an unbelievable jump forward in growth and maturity as she heals.

Neale Walsch says...

> *Illness is not a sign of spiritual weakness, but of spiritual strength. When we fall ill, some will say, "Why did you create that for yourself?*
>
> *They might convince you to see it as a sign of spiritual weakness or failure. It is not. It is a sign of spiritual strength.*
>
> *All challenges are a sign of spiritual strength, and of the readiness of the Soul to move on; to evolve even further.*

In other words, challenges are a cue to release resistance.

Frank, Paul, Mary, Christine, and I each learn to release the past and grow forward through a different experience. Each experience includes pain and sickness

(To clarify, I don't believe pain and sickness are necessary to release resistance. We can certainly release resistance without experiencing pain and sickness. However, I do believe that the only purpose for pain and sickness is to show where the resistance is.)

Each experience brings a greater understanding and an improved lifestyle as we release resistance and increase clarity.

With that clarity, each person moves forward to newer and greater adventures. These adventures would not have been possible without the release of resistance.

As we release resistance, we become generous with our resources. Generosity is the human equivalent of the flow of nature that is necessary for water, fire, wind, and earth to function.

Generosity is necessary for me to experience The Law of Abundance.

Without generosity, I create resistance and block the flow of The Law of Abundance.

Robert releases resistance to the impossible as he travels back to New Mexico from his trip to Vietnam.

He determines that it is time to cash in that battlefield promise made when he flew into a firefight and rescued those ambushed Americans.

He calls and explains the situation. Family members in a closed Communist country want to join family members in the United States.

His friend tells him it won't be easy but "He will see what he can do."

Robert thanks him and ends the call.

These stories provide circumstantial evidence that we move forward every time we release resistance.

Science provides even more evidence for this. I explain this in the following chapters.

In addition, I'll tell you about the result of Robert's phone call.

> **Conspiracy Question**
>
> Have I ever experienced a dramatic release of resistance?
>
> List those experiences.

Chapter 66

The study of vibration explains how we move forward every time we release resistance.

When a possession arrives into my life, I respond in one of three ways.

1. I accept it and share it.
2. I accept it and keep it.
3. I resist it.

These physical acts of sharing, keeping, and resisting have an associated energy.

Since everything is energy and energy travels in waves, the science of vibration explains what happens to my energy when I share, keep, or resist.

SHARING

When a wave travels through space, it gradually loses energy. When I accept something and share it, I add energy to the wave so it can go on to others and bless them.

Generosity accepts the energy and transmits it on so that I experience abundance. In fact, when I give generously, I add energy to what I receive so that the wave goes further.

This is the explanation behind the expression, "Money likes action." Money is a form of energy. When I act, I receive energy, I pass it on, and I experience the benefits. The more I act, the more energy I receive, the more energy I have to pass on and the more benefits I experience.

Action removes things from my life and replaces them with other things. This quick movement attracts more energy. The energy flies into my hands. If I pass it along, I receive the benefits.

When I have too many things, obstacles appear in the form of clutter. These obstacles block the energy. I can only maintain responsibility for so many possessions. When too many items accumulate, there is nowhere to put any new items.

The Law of Abundance continues to work. Possessions continue to come. They gradually weigh me down until I am not able to move. They create a bottleneck.

At this point, delegation becomes a priority. I have to give things away. Sometimes, I give away responsibilities. Sometimes, I give away possessions. Sometimes, I give away money. In every case, I give away the energy I receive so I may receive more.

KEEPING

When a wave travels through space and encounters "soft" or absorbent material, the wave transfers energy to the material and dies.

When I keep something, I take all the energy from the wave. I block the flow with things I already have.

My hoarding, caused by a fear of lack, kills the energy and prevents me from experiencing abundance. When I keep something, I stagnate. More energy attempts to come to me. However, I cannot receive it because I only have so much capacity.

When a dam blocks a river, there has to be spillways and other methods of allowing the water to go downstream. Otherwise, the water will overflow the dam or the dam will break and cause great destruction.

Likewise, I must have releases in my life. Otherwise, when I reach my capacity, the next inflow of energy causes me to overflow. The release of this overflow of energy is usually destructive.

> **Conspiracy Question -**
>
> What clutters my life?

Chapter 67

RESISTING

When a wave travels through space and meets resistance, the wave receives energy to go back in the opposite direction. If the wave source still exists, this amplifies the wave and causes it to grow larger.

When I resist something, I do not kill the wave. I add energy to the wave. This creates conflict and produces guilt and blame.

This resistance prevents me from experiencing other blessings that may come into my life because I cannot accept and resist at the same time.

In addition, I fail at my resistance because anything that comes into my life is there because The Law of Attraction brings it to me.

Once it arrives, I can only try to resist it. However, I can never permanently resist it.

The reason is that it is impossible to accept and resist at the same time. Those two actions are out of integrity with each other. When I resist what comes into my life, I deny reality. The more I resist it, the more it remains.

Whenever I give something attention, it remains. What I resist persists.

It may appear to leave but it doesn't. If it is in my life, I attracted it to myself. The Law of Attraction brought it to me. If I resist it, it will come back stronger the next time. The reason is that I am giving it more attention. I strengthen the energy by resisting it.

Mother Theresa was a woman of peace but she would not attend an anti-war rally. She only attended peace rallies. She understood that resisting something only gives it more energy.

When what I initially resist comes back to me. It is stronger and bigger than before.

I may resist it once, twice, or more and it will continue to come back until it is so big it overwhelms me. At that point, it may be destructive.

Whereas, when I accept it and pass it on the first time it arrives, I experience Peace of Mind because I allow it to flow instead of blocking it.

This is true with every energy form. Water, wind, earth, fire, money, and love work this way.

My gratefulness, even in the face of difficulty, allows me to learn and grow. I then may take that lesson and generously pass it on to others.

I receive Peace of Mind when I express gratefulness through acts of generosity.

I give things away. I pass along everything I can. This is not just giving away items mindlessly. It is the wise acquiring and stewarding of possessions.

Often, there is resistance to giving. I am afraid I will need what I give away. I feel guilty that I'm giving a used item. I blame others for their negative responses to my gift.

The culprits of guilt, blame, and fear show up again and provide resistance. However, when I love, truly love, the guilt, blame, and fear disappear. When I give, I invest into other's Desire. This makes it possible for abundance to flow freely.

In addition, when I give things away, I receive a side benefit. Many of the items I give away are distractions to me. With these distractions out of the way, I am able to focus on my passion.

Without these distractions, I have an abundance of time to enjoy my Desire because I have filtered out the things I don't Desire. I become an expert on my passion. Expertise leads to wealth.

My generosity demonstrates that I have enough. Nobody can steal from me when I'm giving because when someone takes without permission, my attitude of generosity opens the channel wider so The Law of Abundance may replace those items with something better.

If I haven't used something in six months, I give it away. I can always acquire a new item.

When I discover I need something I have given away, I am able to acquire a new item that serves me better. In some cases, people offer me what I need without me having to buy it.

Generous actions reinforce my thoughts and words of gratefulness and open the channel for greater things to come my way.
I habitually look for things to remove from our life. I may sell these items. I may give them away. I may trade for something else. I may throw them away. By doing this, I experience the freedom to see the miracles my heart Desire.

All spiritual teachers emphasize the importance of generosity. They call it tithes. They call it offerings. They call it love gifts. These teachers understand that the emotion of gratefulness expressed in acts of generosity clears the bottleneck in our lives so we can receive new things.

Businesses thrive when they demonstrate generosity. They receive free publicity. They generate good will. Everyone wins in this process.

The Law of Abundance always rewards systems that generate and disperse funds. These systems move the funds without hoarding them.

John Rockefeller, Senior had a net worth of 1.7 billion dollars when he died in spite of giving away 1.3 billion dollars during his lifetime. He developed an entire organization to give away his money.

Bill Gates built great wealth at Microsoft and invested much of that wealth into a foundation. Warren Buffet, one of the wealthiest men of our generation gave most of his wealth to Bill Gates Foundation.

Even with their outrageous generosity, they remain wealthy.

In fact, if you study the lives of wealthy men and women, you will notice an attitude of gratefulness demonstrated by generosity. In all cases, their generosity started before they became wealthy!!

They discovered the key to The Law of Abundance and practiced it in their lives.

My gratefulness in discovering these Laws of the Southwest Lifestyle causes my Desire to share it with you so you may experience the same abundance.

If I don't share, I'm not grateful. If I love what I have, I Desire you to have it.

I Desire for you to experience the same freedoms, joy, and thrills that I have experienced.

That is why I share the Laws of the Southwest Lifestyle. Sharing is the demonstration of the Law of Abundance.

Through sharing, The Law of Abundance provides the fulfillment of my Desire.

Through sharing, The Law of Attraction attracts the sharing that I need.

Through sharing, The Law of Miracles gives me shortcuts in time and space.

> **Conspiracy Question**
>
> How can I immediately demonstrate gratefulness through an act of generosity?
>
> What can I share today?

Chapter 68

I experience all of these laws in my life as I move closer to the fulfillment of my Desire.

That Desire is the one I recognize in the summer of 1984 while attending a seminar in the Baltimore Civic Center. It is the Desire to create a family of fifty people in three generations to make the world a better place.

That fall, I meet a young woman, Sheri. She has a similar Desire and we marry on January 1, 1986.

We add details to our Desire. We decide to have eight children. We decide to be debt free, including our mortgage. We decide to teach our kids at home. That means at least one of us has to work at home.

Almost twelve years later, on a brisk sunny day in the fall of 1997, I write the check for final payment on our mortgage and heave a huge sigh of relief. We are finally debt free. We have no credit card debt, no car payments, and no house payments.

We become debt free while raising seven children and educating them at home. On the day I write that final mortgage check, I feel good about life. We are on our way to fulfilling our Desire.

A little later in that same day, Sheri comes into our home office with a look on her face I have seen several other times. I raise my eyebrows and she nods. We are expecting our eighth child! What an amazing day! Two of our Desires become reality on the same day.

During the next ten years, our eighth child is born. We build our dream house. One of our daughters marries and we become grandparents.

We also meet a remarkable man named Robert.

A few months after Robert makes the call to his friend, he is getting ready for bed when his phone rings.

The voice on the other end identifies himself as a janitor at the Albuquerque International Sunport. A family has just gotten off a plane. They can't speak English. They appear to be Asian.

They have a letter with Robert's name and phone number on it.

The employee wants to know if Robert would be willing to come get them.

Robert picks them up and brings about a wonderful family reunion. He accomplishes the impossible because he works in harmony with The Law of Abundance.

You can accomplish the impossible too when you release all resistance.

As I said earlier…

If you picked up this book looking for financial secrets and money management tips, the material you read may have disappointed you.

I do not apologize for this.

You already know the basics of making and managing money. Anyone can make money.

If anyone can make money, why don't more people make money?

The answer is simple. We know what to do. We just resist doing it.

However, people who don't have enough money and don't have financial peace of mind always have a great deal of resistance in their lives.

In fact, resistance is so ingrained in our society that we will cling to it in the face of great suffering.

I'll say it again.

Most of us would rather live in the security of our poverty than experience the uncertainty of the potential of abundance.

My observation is that if a person understands how to release resistance, he or she can experience abundance.

However, most people are so resistant that no amount of financial instructions can help.

Now that you understand the significance of releasing resistance, I encourage you to continue to release, continue to let go.

This letting go process is necessary for abundance.

This letting go allows you to exit a life of poverty and experience abundance.

I know this because I know that every person has great reserves of energy.

However, instead of using it, we drive in low gear, resistant to shifting gears. If we shifted, we would not only speed up the car. We would do it with far less expenditure of power.

Because the Law of Abundance dictates that Nature is lavish in everything she does, there is abundance for everyone.

This abundance is for you. In fact, the world belongs to you. You are the center of the Universe.

Just as God told Abraham that everything he could see would be his, God tells you that everything is yours.

The Bible says, "Consider the lilies, how they grow."

The flowers, the birds, all of creation, are incessantly active. The trees and flowers in their growth, the birds and wild creatures in building their nests and finding sustenance, are always working and never worrying.

The Universe/God knows what you need and has already sent the supply to you. You may have more than that supply if you simply quit resisting.

Give up worrying, be industrious, and release anxiousness about the outcome.

When you do this, you experience an abundance of resources to fulfill your Desire.

When you do this, you experience financial peace of mind. It is a part of your inward peace. This inward peace brings peace to others. This inward peace brings world peace.

Chapter 69

Q and A about Releasing Resistance

Is it possible for a spiritual presence to cause the physical body to pass out?

Not only is it possible, it is common. I witnessed this phenomenon numerous times in churches throughout the country over the past twenty-five years. In fact, I've spoken in churches, prayed for people, and seen them pass out when I touched their foreheads.

Is this phenomenon unique to Christian churches?

No. My experiences are Christian because of my background. Most other religions report this same phenomenon.

Does the Bible talk about this?

Yes. John Chapter 18 records that it happened to the chief priests and Pharisees when they went to arrest Jesus. Jesus declared who He was and they fell to the ground. There are other instances recorded in the Bible too.

What about when people pass out for other reasons?

Every person I have talked to who passes out has a spiritual story about what they saw during that time. There could be exceptions but I haven't found them.

One person described it as feeling every emotion at once, perfectly balanced.

Does someone have to pass out to experience this?

No, some people experience it during daydreaming or during normal sleep.

Are you saying that sleep is a spiritual experience?

Yes, it can be. Quantum physicists explain it this way: We live in several dimensions at once. The only things that separate us from those different dimensions are space and time. When we sleep, pass out, and daydream, we are traveling outside of time and space. By definition, this is a spiritual experience.

If we experience this daily, then why do some people pass out to experience this?

That's the question I took with me to one of my recent meditation times. The answer I heard was the word, "resistance."

Because we live in a physical body, we resist spiritual teachings. (Look within yourself and I bet you find some resistance to the idea you are reading about now.)

When we are open and things are flowing, we can hear the spiritual messages. However, when we resist, conflict arises. It is like a light bulb in some ways.

The filament's resistance to electrical current provides the glow of a light bulb. Eventually, the filament breaks. The same thing happens to us spiritually. When we resist anything, conflict erupts. We heat up. We glow. We may eventually break (pass out) in order for the resistance to disappear.

Are you saying resistance is always detrimental?

The Law of Attraction says you attract everything into your life. If that is true, your resistance to what arrives means you are against the very thing you attracted. The resistance to what you attracted creates an internal conflict.
At that point, you must release the resistance to have peace.

Does everyone pass out to release the resistance?

Each person doesn't have to pass out to experience the release. You may release it in your nighttime dreams or daydreams. You may release it through some religious ritual. You may need to pass out or go into a coma to experience the release.

Do some people use drugs or alcohol to experience this release?

Yes. I am familiar with Native American religions that use drugs for this purpose. I suspect individuals may use drugs and alcohol for this purpose too.

Are these spiritual messages that important to us?

The great spiritual teachers tell us that the spiritual world is the real world and the physical world is only an illusion. Based on their teachings, the spiritual messages we receive are vital to our well- being.

How do I learn more about the phenomenon?

I suggest you start the process by becoming aware of any resistance you feel. Then, take steps to release it. The important thing isn't how you release the resistance. It is recognizing and removing any resistance from your life.

What is the Next Step on My Journey to Peace of Mind?

The Peace of Mind philosophy taught in *Living the Southwest Lifestyle; How to Have and Maintain Peace of Mind* inspired the development of The Peace of Mind Training Institute, a tax-exempt organization. This training organization offers a variety of resources including workshops, webinars, coaching, books, audios, and videos. There is even an innovative Emissary Program if you decide a Peace of Mind career and business is right for you.

For most people, Peace of Mind Training Institute Workshops featured on the website are the next step. However, if you need individual assistance or have specific questions, we invite you to contact The Peace of Mind Training Institute directly for help in determining which step is right for you.

Website: www.PeaceofMindTrainingInstitute.com
Phone: 505-286-5176
Fax: 505-286-1266
Email: Info@PeaceofMindTrainingInstitute.com
Mailing Address:
    21 Pine Ridge Road,
    Sandia Park NM 87047

Notes

More Information from Living the Southwest Lifestyle

Kokopelli Komments - Profound bits of whimsical wisdom from Kokopelli, an icon of the Southwest. To learn more and register to receive free Kokopelli Komments in your email visit www.ltswls.com and click on the Kokopelli Komment link.

More Books by Matthew C. Cox

Growing Softly Stronger in the Cracked Places
(visit www.softlystronger.com)

www.ingramcontent.com/pod-product-compliance
Lightning Source LLC
Chambersburg PA
CBHW080458110426
42742CB00017B/2931